D1746876

California

Micha Pawlitzki California

EDITION **PANORAMA** BIBLIOTHEK

Kalifornien

Claus Kleber

"Go west, young man!" – im vorletzten Jahrhundert war das Amerikas Mantra, eine zum Ausruf destillierte "manifest destiny", millionenfach wiederholt, in vier Worten die angebliche Bestimmung der weißen Amerikaner, den riesigen Kontinent in Besitz zu nehmen – "from sea to shining sea". An der Küste des Pazifiks, in Kalifornien, hat sich die Bedeutung dieser Worte erschöpft, aber nicht die Energie der Pioniere.

Vielleicht bin ich ja ein bisschen arg romantisch und unverbesserlich Amerika-gläubig, aber ich spüre diese Energie noch, als ich die alte Holztür aufziehe zu "Bucks Restaurant" in Woodside, einem Nest in den kieferbestandenen Hügeln über Silicon Valley. Jamis McNiven, ein hünenhafter Ex-Hippie im schreiend bunten Seidenhemd, die mittlerweile grauen Haare lang nach hinten gekämmt, herrscht über die wahrscheinlich produktivste Dorfkneipe der Welt. An den Resopal-Tischen sitzen die Gäste zu früher Stunde vor herzhaften Portionen Rühreiern, Speck und Avocado-Salat. Man muss schon sehr sorgfältig hinschauen, auf Tischmanieren und Shirt-Marken achten, um die Gäste einordnen zu können. Da sind Banker, Bauern, Investoren, Erfinder. Jamis wogt zwischen den Tischen hin und her und verkuppelt, was zusammen gehört. In seiner Kneipe wurde "www.hotmail" gegründet und "ebay". Und auch die beiden Gründer von "yahoo" waren hier, die mit ihrer Idee für eine Internet-Suchmaschine zweimal beim selben Investor abblitzten – „der beißt sich heute noch in den Hintern" lacht Jamis. Natürlich wurde an seinen Tischen auch schon eine Menge Geld verbrannt, in hoffnungslose Träume investiert. Wie das so ist im Goldrausch. In Kalifornien ist der nie vorüber gewesen, er ist zum Stoßfieber geworden, das seit dem Fund der ersten Nuggets im Sacramento River 1848 immer wieder kommt. Edelmetalle, Landwirtschaft, Rüstungsindustrie, Autos, Immobilien, Computer, Software, das erste Internet, dann Web 2.0. Immer wieder ging es steil nach oben, auch immer wieder abwärts, aber unter dem Strich wies Kaliforniens Lebenskurve anderthalb Jahrhunderte lang nach oben – und vor allem nach vorne, wie es sich für den Staat der Pioniere gehört.

Dort vorne sehen Jamis und seine Gäste die nächste Welle kommen und sind fest entschlossen, auf ihr zu surfen: Green Industry. „Ein Tsunami von Dollars geht in Windkraft, Solarstrom und moderne, leistungsstarke Batterien" sagt mir der Investmentbanker Bill Reicker, der neben einem großen "Mug" schwachen Kaffees Texte abwechselnd in Telefon und Laptop hackt und auf sein "date" wartet, die ihm etwas über eine Idee zur energiesparenden Vernetzung von Kraftwerken erzählen will. Bills Auftraggeber sind heiß auf solche Projekte. Und Jamis, dem alten Hippie, lacht das Herz. Wenn man auf einen Schlag Geld verdienen, Spaß haben und die Welt retten kann, bleiben keine Wünsche offen. It's the ultimate Californian dream. Schließlich ist Jamis – wie damals so viele seiner Generation – nicht nur für freizügigen Sex und bewusstseinserweiternde Drogen von der Ostküste nach Kalifornien getrampt, sondern auch wegen der Natur, die dieses Buch in herrlichen Bildern feiert.

Der zwölfhundert Kilometer lange, vierhundert Kilometer breite Streifen am Pazifik ist ein Riegel aus Paradiesen. Die Hügel und Canyons von Malibu bei Los Angeles, das fruchtbare Sacramento Valley, die schroffe Küste von Big Sur zwischen San Simeon und Carmel im Norden, die atemberaubende Berglandschaft des Yosemite National Park, die endlose Weite der Sierra Nevada, die Redwood Forests im Norden an der Grenze zu Oregon und das Napa Valley bei San Francisco, das ertragreichste Weingebiet der Welt. Kaum ein anderer Bundesstaat hat mehr National Monuments und Nationalparks. Selbst Kaliforniens Wüsten sind Naturwunder: In einer von ihnen, der Mojave Desert, der trockensten Wüste der Welt, findet man im Death Valley den tiefgelegensten Punkt Nordamerikas, während der 4418 m hohe Mount Whitney in der Sierra Nevada der höchste Berg der USA außerhalb Alaskas ist.

Ich bin auf den Highways und By-Ways Kaliforniens nie lange gefahren, ohne in Woody Guthrie's "This Land is Your Land, this Land is My Land" auszubrechen – laut und falsch. Dabei ist es über weite Strecken Wahnsinn, dass hier Menschen siedeln. Wer ist nur auf den Gedanken gekommen, Los Angeles, eine der größten Städte der Welt, in die Wüste und zudem auf einen tektonischen Graben zu setzen, der mit tödlicher Sicherheit irgendwann – vielleicht schon in Minuten – ein neues, verheerendes Erdbeben produzieren wird? "The Big One", eine Erschütterung, deren Folgen und Kosten sich niemand ausmalen will. Kalifornien wäre auch nicht der reichste Farmstaat Amerikas, wenn sich die frühen Geschäftemacher nicht das Recht ergaunert hätten, den Colorado, den roten Fluss, auszubluten. Der liebe Gott, nach weitverbreiteter Überzeugung jemand aus Kalifornien, hat dieses Stück Erde nicht als bevölkerungsreichsten Staat der USA vorgesehen, soviel steht fest. Die Menschen haben ihren Lebensraum und Lebensstil der Schöpfung abgetrotzt, das kann nicht ewig gut gehen. Scheinbar alle paar Wochen erinnern Trockenheiten, Überschwemmungen, Waldbrände, Bergrutsche und Erdbeben daran. Seltsam, dass sich ausgerechnet unter dieser Dauerbedrohung ein "California Spirit" entwickelt hat, der im Spektrum der Emotionen und Lebenseinstellungen ziemlich am anderen Ende vom deutschen Gemüt steht. Hier gilt in allen Krisen eine typisch kalifornische Weisheit, die in deutschen Ohren schön, aber unrealistisch klingt: heute ist besser als gestern, aber bestimmt nicht so gut wie morgen.

Der Gedanke ist ansteckend, über alle nationalen, ethnischen, religiösen Grenzen hinweg. In den Straßen von San Francisco, den Universitäten von Berkeley, Stanford und LA, auf den Campus von Apple und Google erlebe ich eine UN der Talente, in der Hautfarbe, Herkunft und die jeweilige Façon selig zu werden keine trennenden Merkmale mehr sind. Die Kommando-Brücke des Raumschiffs Enterprise, der Hollywood-Traum von einem Team aus Menschen und Aliens, die ihre unterschiedlichen Arten zu denken und handeln zum gemeinsamen Nutzen einsetzen, ist in Kalifornien an vielen Stellen längst Wirklichkeit geworden. Es gibt immer noch gewaltige Spannungen zwischen Rassen und sozialen Klassen, aber gleichzeitig wird produktive Gemeinsamkeit vorgelebt. Ein europäischer Défätist, der da noch zweifelt, ob sich das Bessere am Ende wirklich durchsetzen wird.

Kaliforniens multikulturelle "work force" erfindet zurzeit die Industrie der Zukunft, eine "knowledge-industry", die keine Grenzen mehr kennt. Silicon Valley hat ihr mit den Internet-Suchmaschinen von Yahoo bis Google und Cuil die Werkzeuge in die Hand gegeben. Damit machen sie sich jetzt an die Probleme des 21. Jahrhunderts.

Dabei verlässt man sich beileibe nicht nur auf "local talent". Wie ein Magnet scheint Kalifornien wagemutige und innovative Köpfe von überall her anzuziehen. Martin Roscheisen, ein gebürtiger Münchner ist da nur eines von vielen Beispielen. Er hat in Stanford studiert und eine Software entwickelt, auf der die "social websites" wie facebook.com und studivz.de beruhen. Das Geld, das er damit verdient hat, wird er auch bei verschwenderischster Lebensführung nie mehr ausgeben können. Aber Multimillionär sein war ihm schon nach ein paar Monaten zu langweilig. Er beschloss, sich um das neue, heiße Thema in Silicon Valley zu kümmern: Solarenergie. Das sind vor allem Probleme der Elektronik, Materialwissenschaften, Kristallforschung – von nichts davon hatte er auch nur einen blassen Schimmer. Aber Stanford hatte ihn gelehrt, Probleme zu analysieren, konkrete Fragen zu formulieren und Antworten zu suchen. Vor allem aber, wie er lachend sagt, vor keiner Herausforderung Respekt zu haben. Gemeinsam mit einer handvoll Freunde reiste er rund um die Welt in alle Labors, die auf diesem Gebiet von sich reden machten. Sie steckten alle in derselben Sackgasse: die Produktivität der Solarzellen ließ sich nicht mehr wesentlich steigern, kaum noch mehr Strom herausholen. So entschloss sich der tatendurstige, aber ahnungslose Deutsche aus Silicon Valley, stattdessen die Herstellung billiger zu machen. Viel billiger. Aus diesem Ziel ergaben sich Dutzende von schwierigen technischen Fragen. Roscheisen und seine Partner durchforsteten das world wide web nach dem passenden Know-how. Ein entscheidender Durchbruch gelang, als sie in Kontakt mit einem Materialwissenschaftler aus der äußeren Mongolei gerieten. Am Ende stand ein Verfahren, das Solarzellen auf schlichte Alufolie druckt wie Buchstaben auf Zeitungspapier. Die Herstellungskosten sollen um 85% sinken. Die Investoren stehen mit zweistelligen Millionenbeträgen Schlange.

Als wir Roscheisen und sein Team im Labor besuchen, spritzen die Testmaschinen noch wirre, fleckige Muster auf die Folie, aber ein paar Meilen weiter, in der hundert Meter langen Fabrikationshalle, werden schon die gewaltigen Druckstraßen installiert, die sofort mit der Massenproduktion beginnen sollen, sobald die letzten Probleme gelöst sind. In Deutschland hätten wohl noch monatelang Fachleute und Prüfausschüsse ihre Spezifikationen definiert und Banker nachdenklich mit den Köpfen gewackelt, bevor die teuren Maschinen bestellt werden durften. Roscheisen und seine Investoren „went for home", was in der amerikanischen Baseballsprache nicht den Feierabend ankündigt, sondern einen irren Lauf aufs Ganze – bis ins Ziel.

Es wäre nicht das erste Mal, dass kalifornische Energie deutschen Ingenieuren den Vorsprung wieder abnimmt, den sie mühsam erarbeitet haben. Diesmal in Umwelt-Technologien.

Auch auf dieses Thema ist Kalifornien auf kalifornische Weise gekommen. Ich wollte es zunächst nicht glauben, habe es aber so oft und von so vielen gesagt bekommen, dass ich nun keine Zweifel mehr habe. Es war ein Produkt aus Hollywood, das die Augen und die Geldschleusen öffnete: Al Gores Film über „Eine unbequeme Wahrheit". Der verfilmte Dia-Abend des gescheiterten Präsidentschaftskandidaten enthielt fast nichts, was einem durchschnittlichen Fernsehzuschauer neu gewesen wäre, aber so geschickt aufbereitet, mit Star-Value verkauft und mit Oscar und Friedensnobelpreis geadelt, brachte es die Nachbarn der Traumfabrik zum Handeln. Seitdem suchen nicht mehr nur die Erfinder nach Geld, sondern Milliarden Risiko-Kapital suchen händeringend nach brauchbaren Ideen. Viele werden ihr Geld verlieren – und wir werden nur von den Gewinnern hören, die die Welt verändern. Das werden hier alle ganz in Ordnung finden – auch die Verlierer. Solange die Erneuerer aus Kalifornien kommen. Wie schon so oft.

In den sechziger Jahren begann in Kalifornien die Studentenbewegung gegen ungebremsten Kapitalismus und den Vietnamkrieg, inspiriert von den Schriften eines deutschen Philosophen. Herbert Marcuse lehrte damals in San Diego. Bald versuchten Männer wie der zukünftige Gouverneur Jerry Brown, (für Amerika) aufregend linke Positionen der gereiften Hippies in konkrete Politik zu formen. In den siebziger Jahren des letzten Jahrhunderts kamen auch die ersten Umweltgesetze gegen die Autoindustrie aus Kalifornien, vom Zwang zum Katalysator bis zu Obergrenzen für Flottenverbräuche, die in Europa bis heute nicht durchgesetzt werden konnten.

Chancen für Außenseiter und ungewöhnliche Ideen sind aber kein alleiniges Privileg der Linken. Auch die Reagan-Revolution mit ihrer einer aus Kalifornien selbstbewussten Haltung gegenüber dem „Reich des Bösen" kam aus Kalifornien.

Heute steht – mit anderen Antworten auf andere Fragen – Arnold Schwarzenegger in dieser Tradition. Er ritt auf einer beispiellos geschickt gesteuerten, populistischen Welle ins Amt. Und hätte gute Chancen, seinem Vorbild Reagan auch den letzten Schritt ins Weiße Haus zu folgen, wenn das nicht eine antiquierte (und sehr unkalifornische) Regelung in der Bundesverfassung für im Ausland geborene Bürger unmöglich machte. Er hat immer noch seinen harten österreichischen Akzent, aber das macht nichts, solange er für kalifornisches Selbstbewusstsein steht. Ich war dabei, als er in einen Saal rief: „Wir sind Amerika. Nicht Washington. Washington ist nichts weiter als ein Klecks auf der Landkarte". Tosender Beifall dankte es ihm. Sein Staat verkörpert den amerikanischen Traum nicht unbedingt besser, aber selbstbewusster als andere.

Thomas Jefferson, der so poetisch die amerikanische Unabhängigkeitserklärung formulierte, war ein belesener Landadliger aus Virginia. Er konnte wunderbar schreiben über die von Gott gegebene Rechte auf Leben und Freiheit, aber den schönsten Satz, den vom Menschenrecht auf das Streben nach Glück, muss ihm ein Engel aus Kalifornien eingeflüstert haben.

California

Claus Kleber

"Go west, young man!" – in the 19th Century, this was America's mantra, a "manifest destiny", distilled into a call, repeated millions of times, in four words the appointed task of the white Americans to take possession of the vast continent - "from sea to shining sea". While, this mission reached its natural limits on the shores of the Pacific, the pioneer's energy remained boundless..

Perhaps I am just a little romantic and a confirmed believer in America, but I still sense this energy as I open the old wooden door to "Buck's Restaurant" in Woodside, a nest in the pine-covered hills above Silicon Valley. Jamis McNiven, a gigantic ex-hippie in a screamingly loud silk shirt, his now grey hair combed far to the back, runs what is probably the most productive country diner in the world. From the early hours, the guests sit at the Resopal tables in front of generous platefuls of scrambled eggs, bacon and avocado salad. One has to look very carefully, and pay attention to the table manners and the shirt tags, in order to be able to classify the guests. Here are bankers, farmers, investors and inventors. Jamis weaves to and fro between the tables, putting together what goes together: "www.hotmail" and "ebay" were both founded here in his diner. The two founders of "yahoo" were also here, twice getting the brush-off from the same investor with their idea for an Internet search engine – "that guy must still be kicking himself today" laughs Jamis. A great deal of money has of course also been lost at his tables, invested in hopeless dreams. This is always the way with gold fever. In California, this has never been cured, and has become an endemic disease which has returned time and time again ever since the discovery of the first nuggets in the Sacramento River in 1848. Precious metals, agriculture, the armaments industry, cars, property, computers, software, the first Internet, and then Web 2.0. The sharp upturn has always been followed by a downturn, but on balance, California's star has always been in the ascendant over the last century and a half, and above all looking forward, as is only fitting for the pioneer state.

Now, Jamis and his guests see the next wave coming, and are firmly determined to surf it: Green industry. "A tsunami of dollars is going into wind power, solar energy and modern, high-performance batteries", as I am told by the investment banker Bill Reicker, sitting in front of a large mug of weak coffee, and alternately tapping texts into his telephone and laptop while waiting for his "date", who wants to tell him something about an idea for the energy-saving networking of power stations. Bill's clients are eagerly awaiting such projects. And Jamis, the old hippie, is also bounding with enthusiasm. If you can make money, have fun and save the world all in one go, what more could you want. It's the ultimate Californian dream. After all, Jamis – like so many others of his generation at the time – came from the east coast to California not only for free love and awareness-enhancing drugs, but also because of the nature celebrated by the magnificent pictures in this book.

The 750 mile long and 250 mile wide coastal plain bordering the Pacific is made up of one paradise after the other. The hills and canyons of Malibu near Los Angeles, the fertile Sacramento Valley, the rocky coastline of Big Sur between San Simeon in the south and Carmel in the north, the breathtaking mountain landscape of the Yosemite National Park, the endless wastes of the Sierra Nevada, the Redwood forests in the north on the border with Oregon and the Napa Valley near San Francisco, the most productive vine-growing area in the world. Hardly any other state in the USA has more national monuments and national parks. Even California's deserts are wonders of nature: In one of them, the Mojave Desert, the most arid desert in the world, lies the deepest point in North America – Death Valley, while the 14,500 ft. Mount Whitney in the Sierra Nevada is the highest mountain in the USA outside Alaska.

I have never driven for long on the highways and byways of California without breaking out into Woody Guthrie's "This land is your land, this land is my land" – very loudly and very badly. In many places, it seems to be absolute lunacy for people to have settled here. Whoever came up with the idea of building Los Angeles, today one of the largest cities in the world, in the middle of the desert, and what is more right above a geological fault, which sooner or later, and with deadly certainty – perhaps even minutes from now – will produce yet another devastating earthquake? "The Big One", a quake whose consequences and costs nobody even wants to imagine. California would also not be the richest farming state in America if the early wheeler-dealers had not wangled for themselves the right to tap the Colorado, the Red River. The Lord God, widely believed to come from California, never intended this parcel of land to become the most populous state of the USA, so much is certain. The people here have wrested their living space and lifestyle from creation, but this cannot always remain so. Every few weeks, droughts, floods, forest fires, mountain landslides and earthquakes provide unpleasant reminders to this effect. It is strange that particularly under this permanent threat, a "California spirit" has developed, which in the spectrum of emotions and attitudes to life appears diametrically opposed to that of the German disposition. Here a typical Californian saying applies in all crises, which may sound fine to European ears, although rather unrealistic: today is better than yesterday, but certainly not as good as tomorrow.

The thought is infectious, transcending all national, ethnic and religious boundaries. In the streets of San Francisco, the universities of Berkeley, Stanford and LA, on the campus of Apple and Google, I experience here a united nation of talents in which skin colour, origin and the relevant means of being happy are no longer distinguishing features. The bridge of the starship Enterprise, the Hollywood dream of a team of people and aliens, who apply their different ways of thinking and acting for the common good, has long been reality in many places in California. Great tensions still exist between races and social classes, but at the same time productive solidarity is also practised. A European defeatist, who still doubts whether the better will really prevail in the end.

California's multi-cultural work force is currently inventing the industry of the future, a "knowledge industry" which knows no bounds. Silicon Valley has given it the tools to do the job with the Internet search engines of Yahoo to Google and Cuil, and they are now putting them to work to solve the problems of the 21st Century.

And they are by no means relying only on "local talent". California seems to attract venturous and innovative people from all over the world like a magnet. Martin Roscheisen, a native of Munich, is only one of many examples. He studied in Stanford and developed a software on which the "social websites" such as facebook.com and studivz.de are based. He will never be able to spend all the money he earned from this, even with the most lavish lifestyle. But being a multimillionaire became too boring for him, even after a few months. He decided to get involved with the new, hot topic of Silicon Valley: solar energy. These consist primarily of problems of electronics, materials sciences and crystal research – all subjects of which he had not the faintest idea.

But Stanford had taught him to analyse problems, formulate concrete questions and then look for the answers. Above all however, as he says laughingly, not to harbour respect for any challenge. Together with a handful of friends, he travelled round the world to every laboratory which had made a name for itself in this field. They had all come to the same dead-end: the productivity of solar cells could no longer be increased significantly, there was no more electricity to be obtained. So, without any ideas but thirsting for action, the German from Silicon Valley decided instead to make their production cheaper. Much cheaper. This goal threw up dozens of difficult technical questions. Roscheisen and his partners scoured the worldwide web for the relevant know-how. A decisive breakthrough was achieved when they made contact with a materials scientist from Outer Mongolia. This ultimately resulted in a process which prints solar cells onto simple aluminium film, like letters onto newsprint. The production cost should fall by 85%. The investors are queuing up, each with tens of millions of dollars in their hands.

When we visited Roscheisen and his team in the laboratory, the test machines were still spraying confused, mottled patterns onto the film, but a few miles further on, in the 100 metre long production shop, the huge printing lines were already being installed, ready to start mass production immediately, as soon as the last teething problems have been solved. In Germany, specialists and test committees would probably have taken months just to define their specifications, while bankers cautiously shook their heads, before these expensive machines could have been ordered. Roscheisen and his investors "went for home", which in American baseball jargon does not mean finishing work for the day, but making a mad dash to achieve the objective.

It would not be the first time that Californian energy had stolen from German engineers the lead they had gained so laboriously – this time in environmental technologies.

California also arrived at this subject in a Californian way. I didn't want to believe it at first, but have heard it so often and from so many people that I no longer have any doubt. It was a product of Hollywood which opened people's eyes, and the investors' purses: Al Gore's film about "An inconvenient truth". The filmed presentation of the failed presidential candidate contains almost nothing which would have been new to the average TV viewer, but it was prepared so slickly, marketed with star value and honoured with an Oscar and the Nobel peace prize that it brought the neighbours of the dream factory to the point of action. Since then, the inventors have no longer been looking for money, although investors with billions in risk capital have been wringing their hands in the search for usable ideas. Many will lose their money – and we will hear only of the winners who are changing the world. All the people here will find this quite in order – even the losers. As long as the innovators come from California, as so often the case.

The student movement against unbridled capitalism and the Vietnam War began in the 1960's in California, inspired by the writings of a German philosopher. Herbert Marcuse was teaching at the time in San Diego. Soon, men like the future Governor Jerry Brown were trying to turn the (for America) strikingly left-wing positions of the mature hippies into concrete policies. In the 1970's, the first environmental legislation against the automotive industry also originated from California, from compulsory catalytic converters to upper limits for vehicle fleet fuel consumption, regulations which have been impossible to implement in Europe to the present day.

Opportunities for outsiders and unusual ideas are however not the sole privilege of the left. The Reagan revolution with its intransigent, almost arrogantly self-confident attitude towards the "evil empire" also originated in California.

This tradition is being continued today by Arnold Schwarzenegger – with different answers to different questions. He came into office on a masterfully controlled popularist wave, and would have had a good chance of following his model Reagan the final step into the White House, if this had not been made impossible for citizens not born in the USA by an antiquated (and very un-Californian) stipulation in the Constitution. He still has his pronounced Austrian accent, but that doesn't matter, as long as he stands up for Californian self-confidence. I was there when he proclaimed: "We are America. Not Washington. Washington is nothing more than a dot on the map", to the tumultuous applause of the audience. His state embodies the American dream, not necessarily better, but more self-confidently than others.

Thomas Jefferson, who formulated the American declaration of Independence so poetically, was a well-read landowner from Virginia. He could write wonderfully about God-given rights to life and liberty, but the most beautiful phrase about the human right to the pursuit of happiness must have been whispered in his ear by an angel from California.

Beach near Sonoma Coast 1

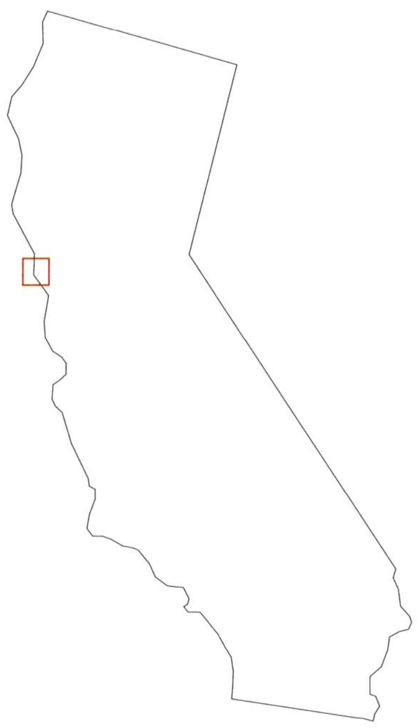

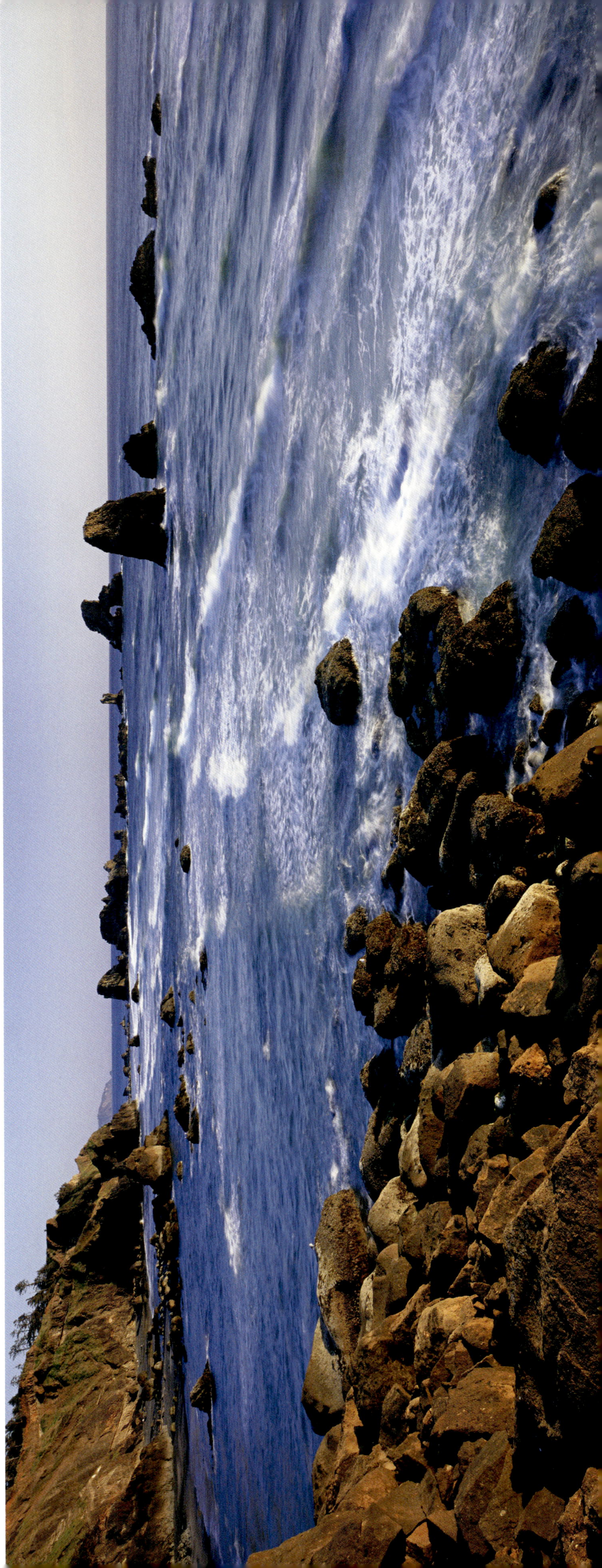

Beach on Sonoma Coast 2

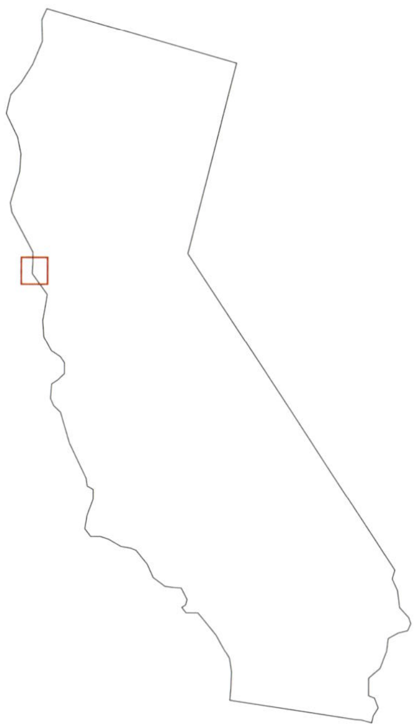

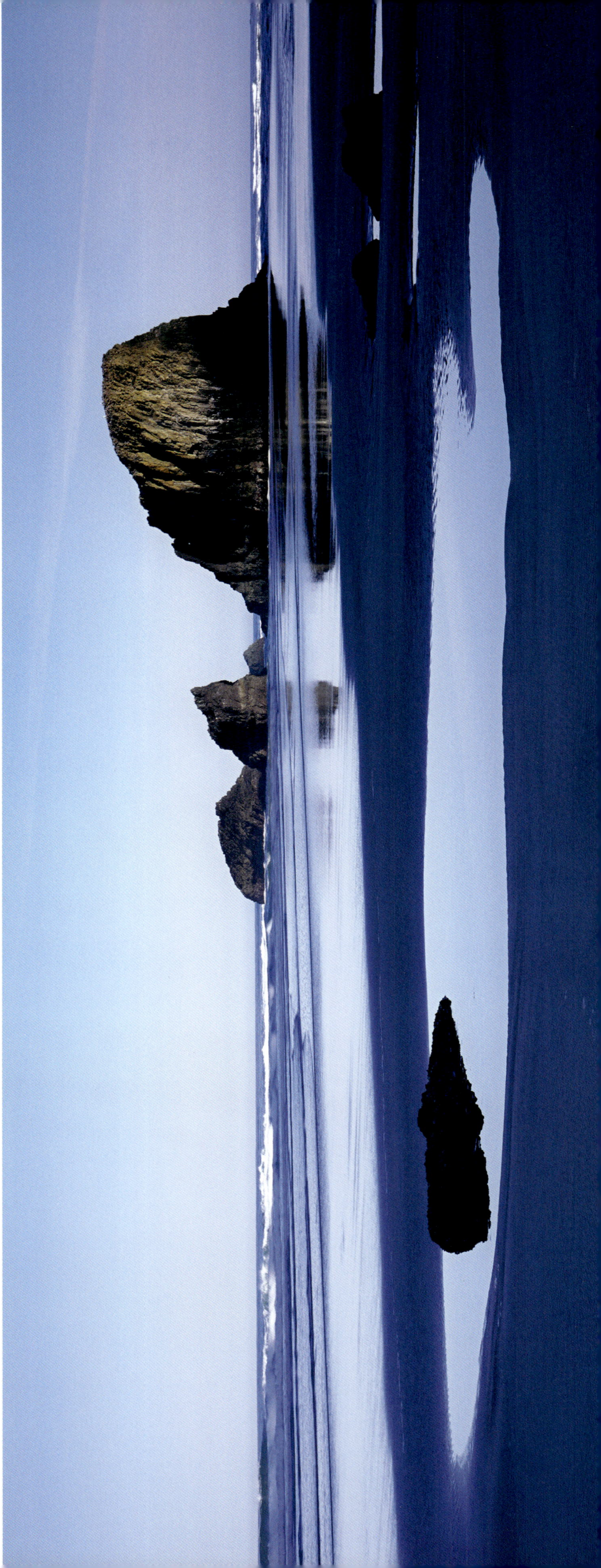

Route 66 near Mojave Desert 3

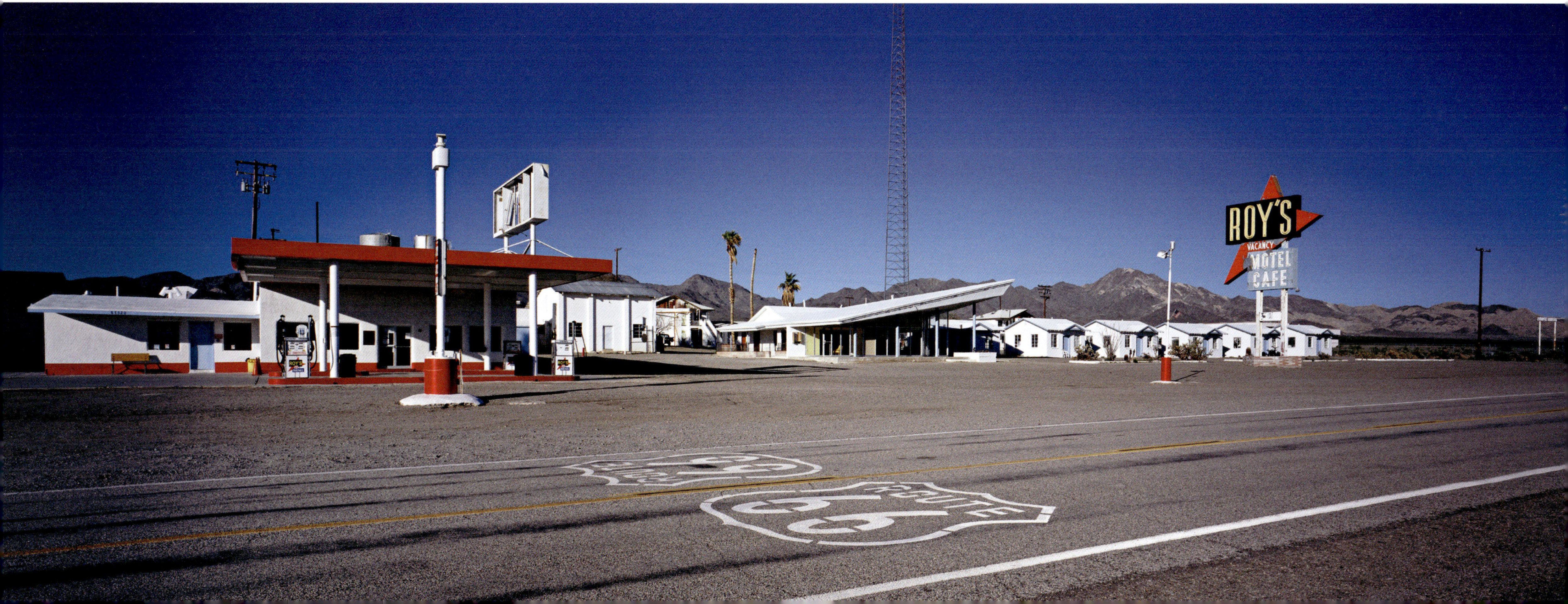
ROY'S
VACANCY
MOTEL
CAFE
ROUTE
66

Indian petroglyphs, Owens Valley 4

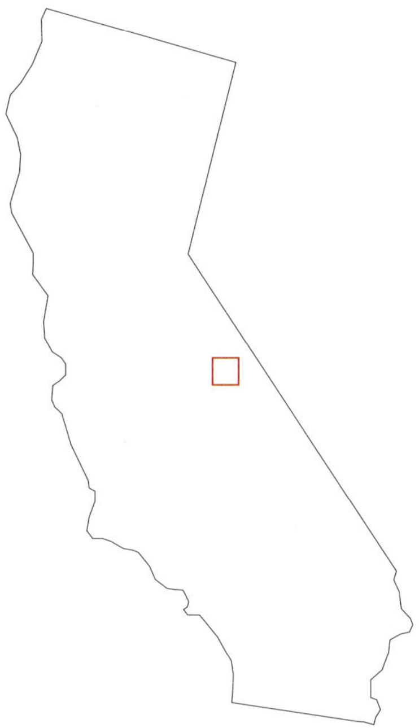

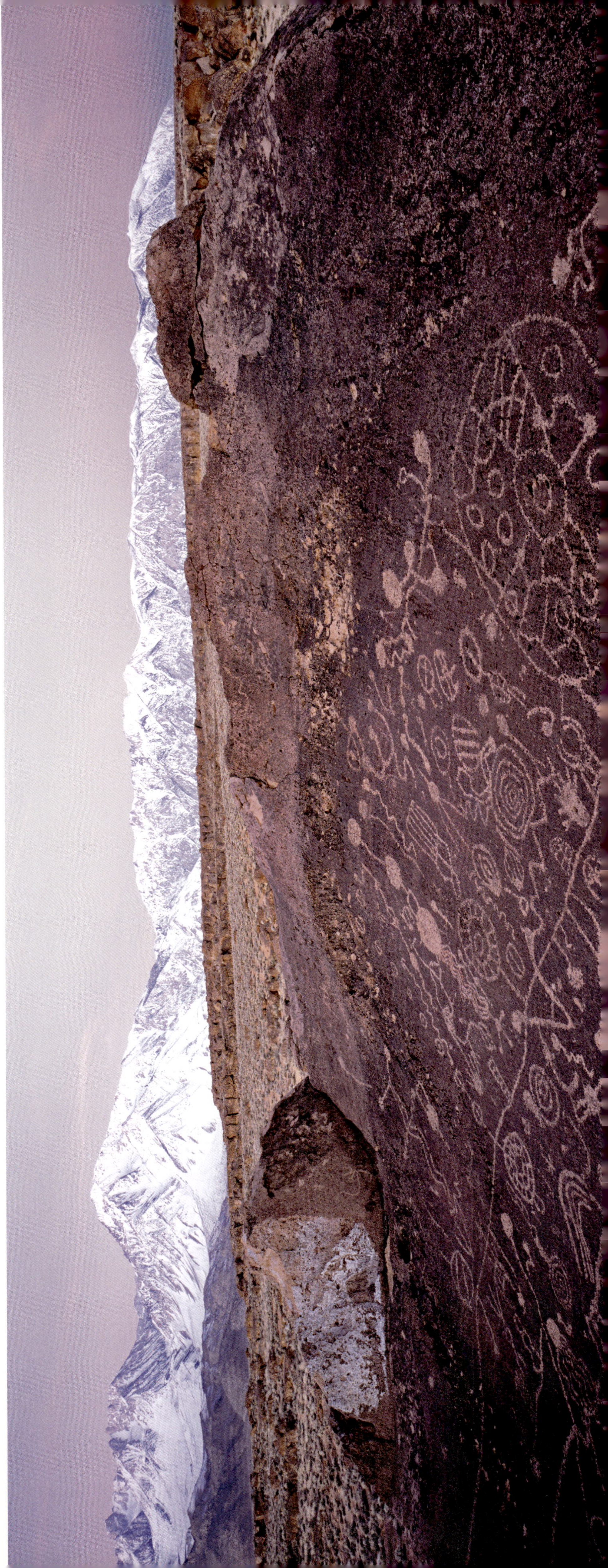

Redwood National Park 5

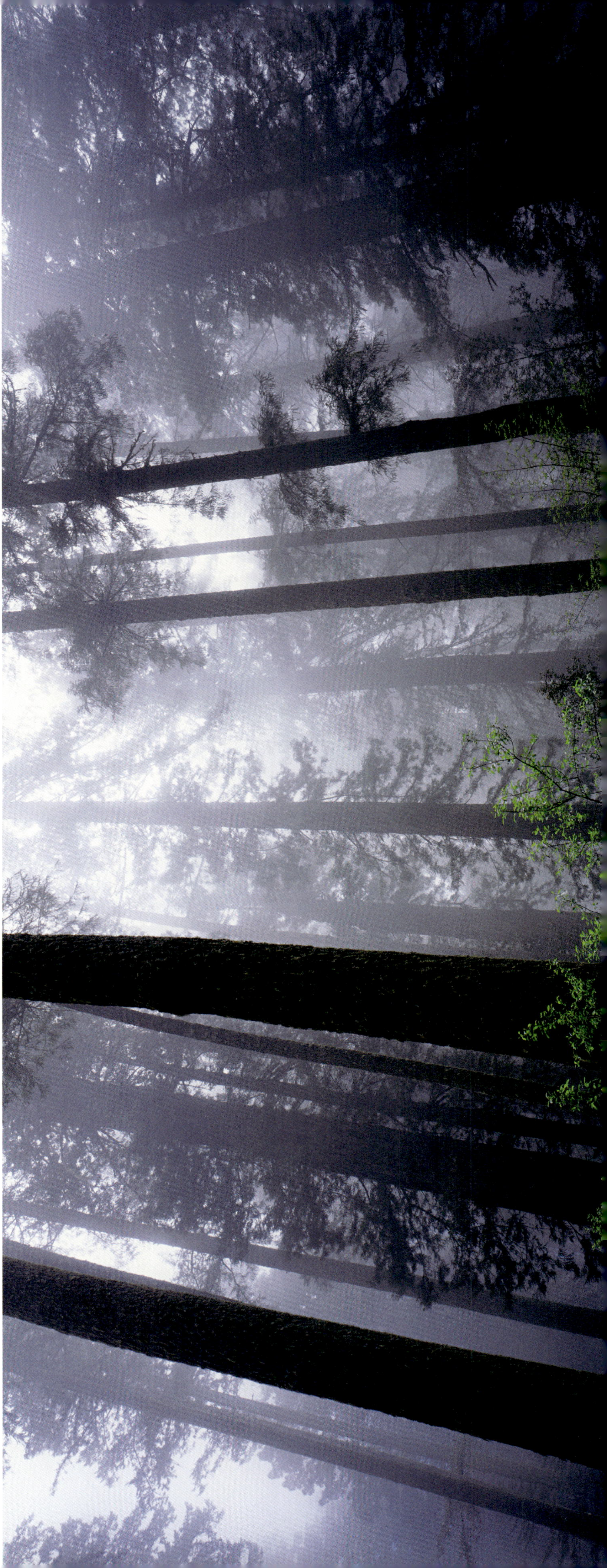

White Mountains, Ancient Bristlecone Pine Forest 6

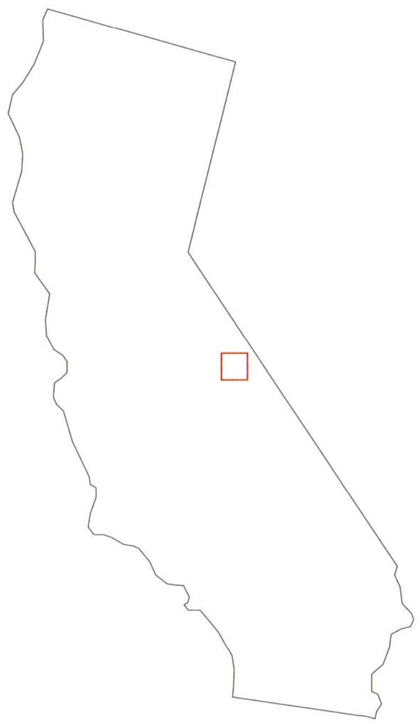

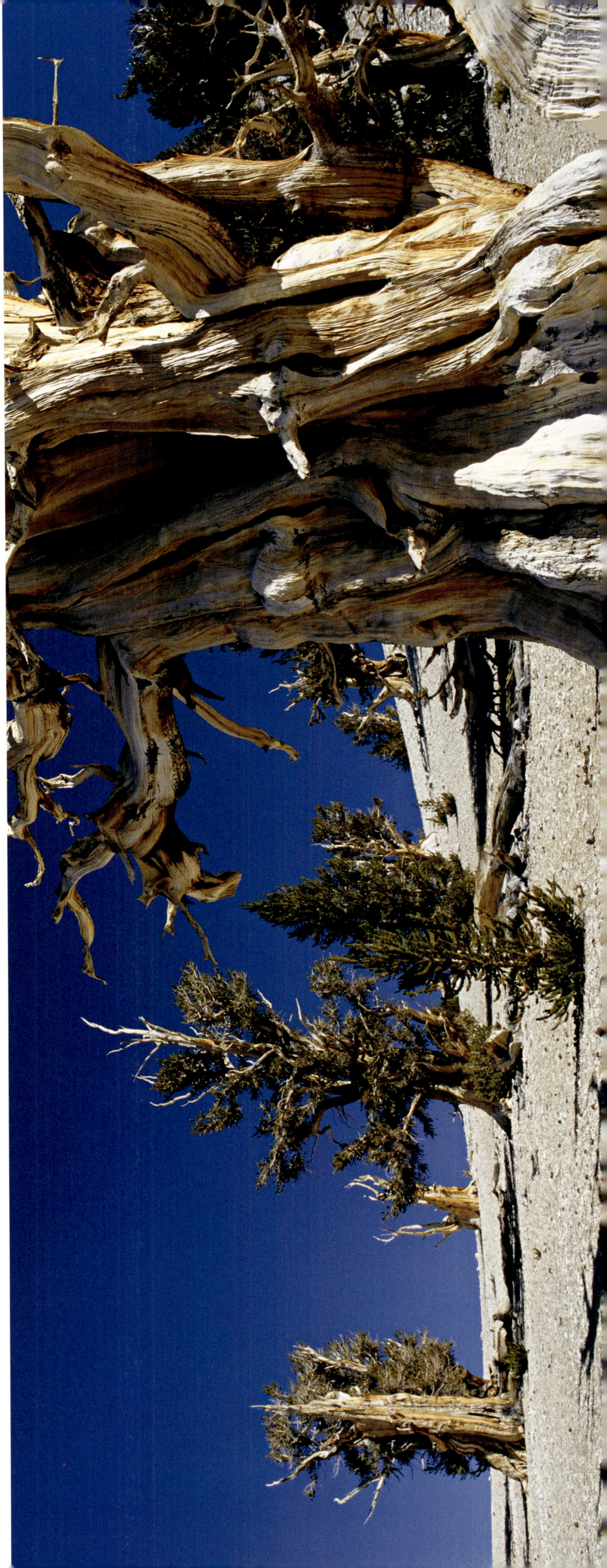

7

Mono Lake

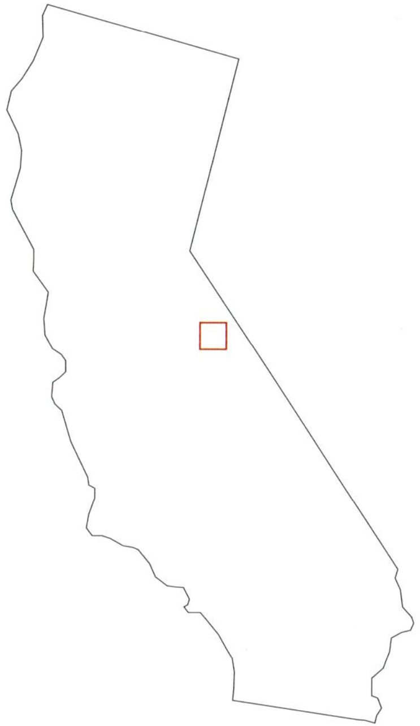

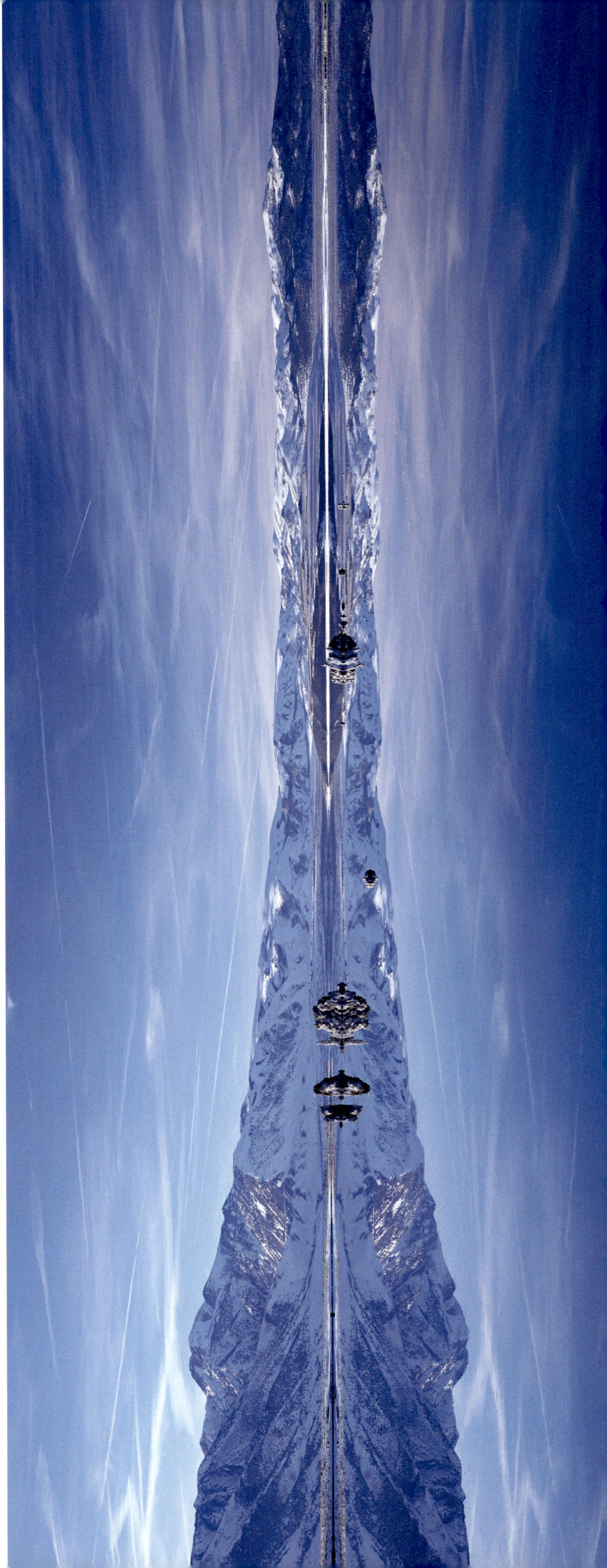

8

Mono Lake

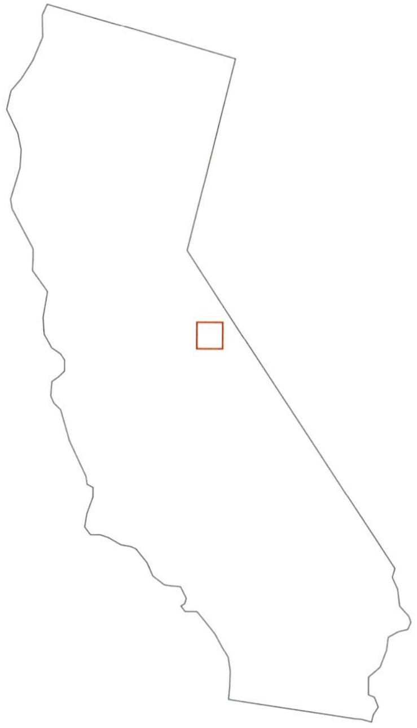

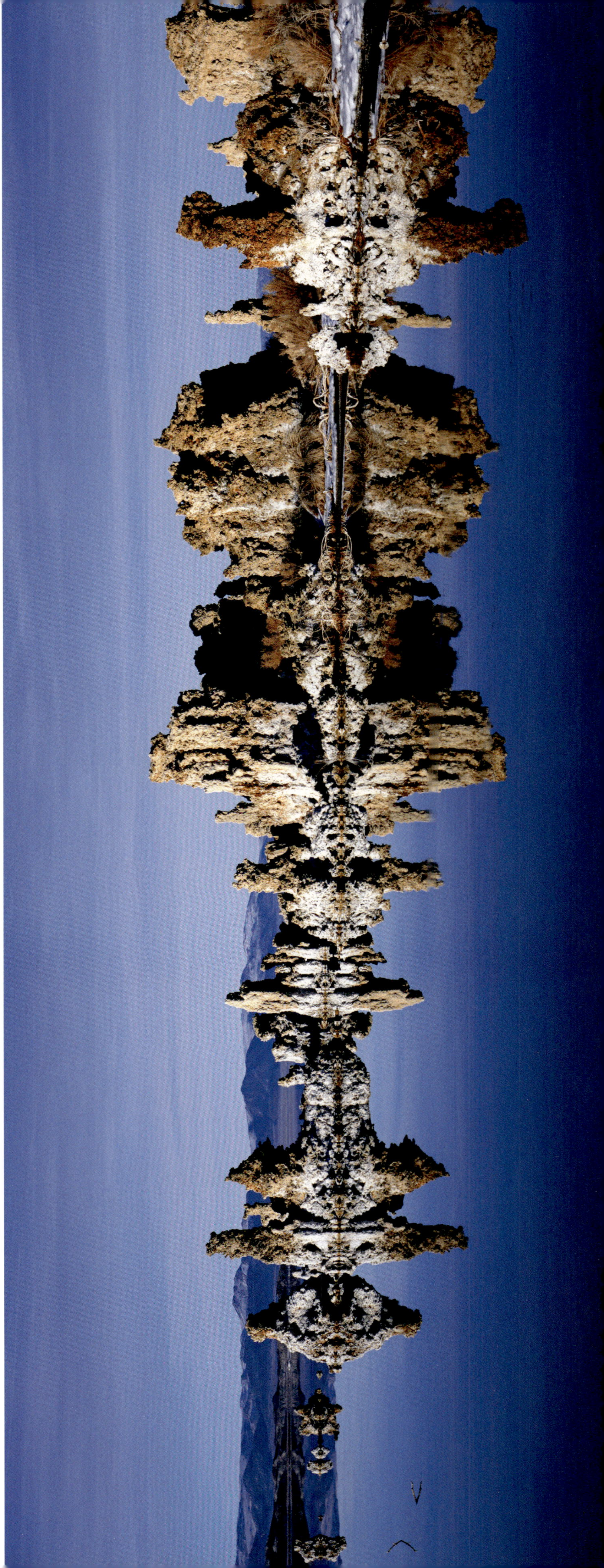

Golden Gate Bridge, San Francisco 9

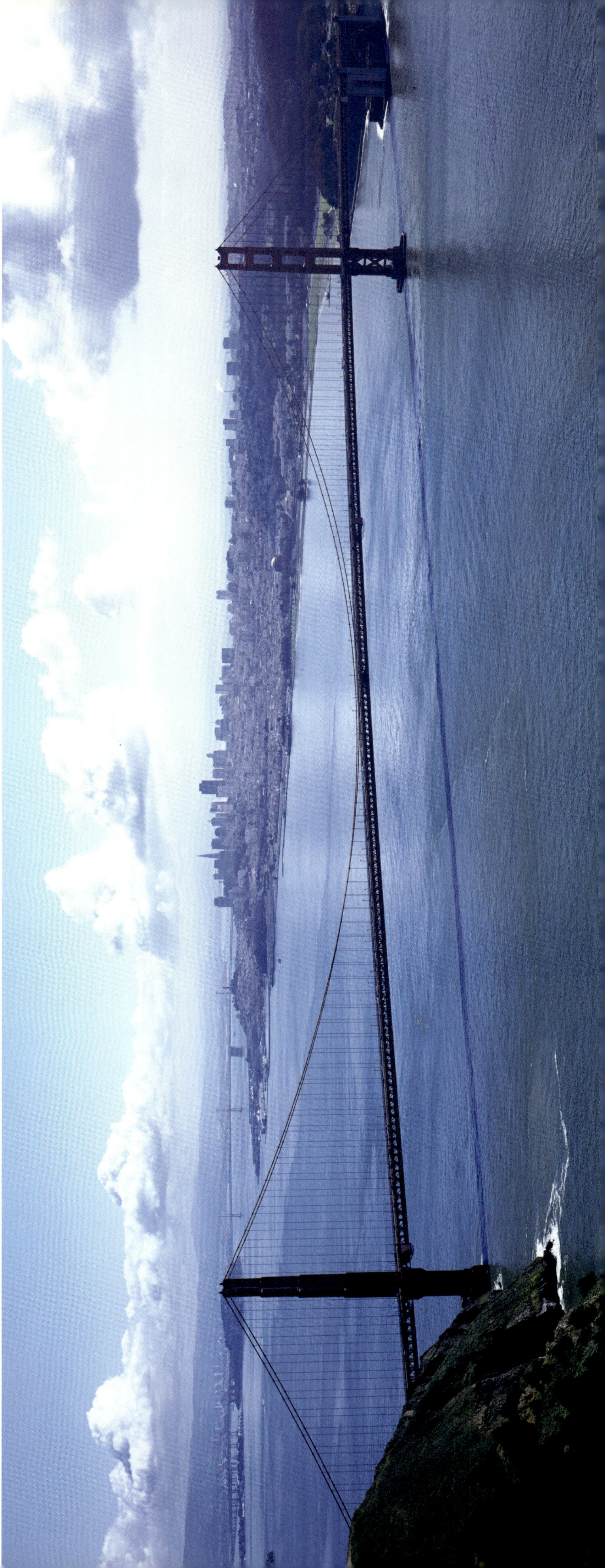

Downtown San Francisco 10

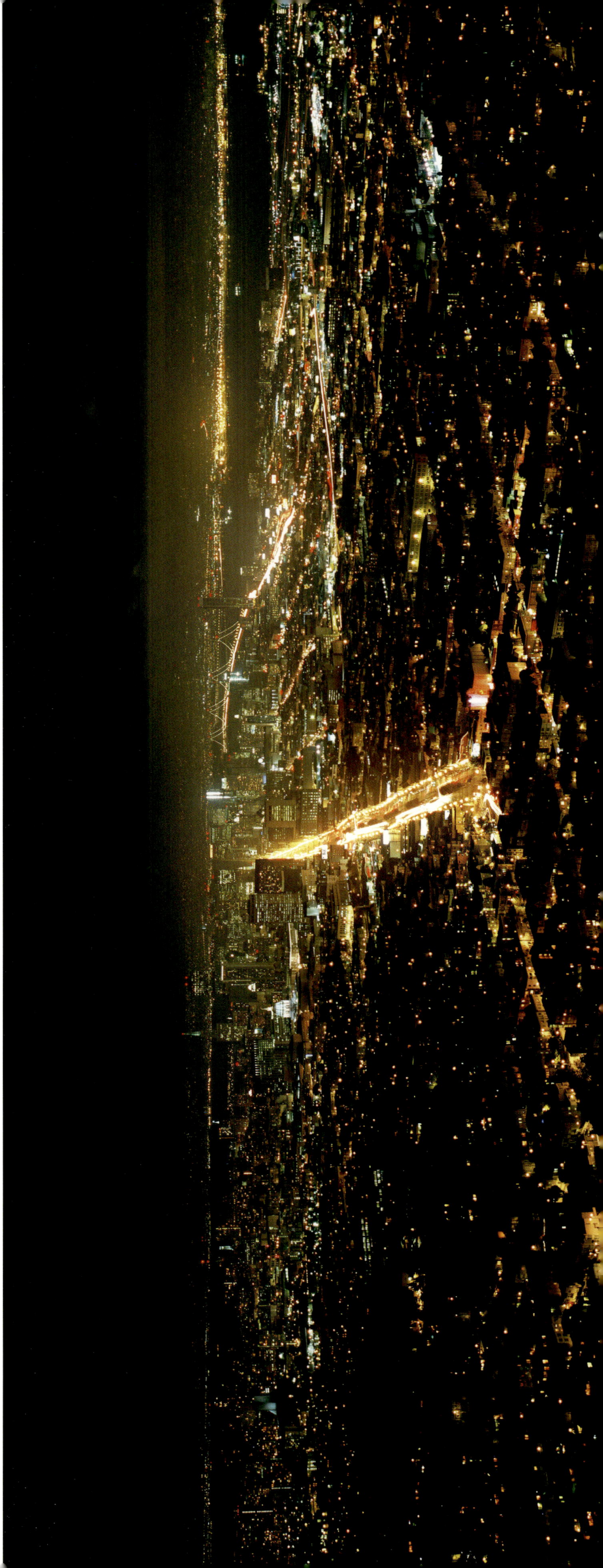

"Painted Ladies", San Francisco

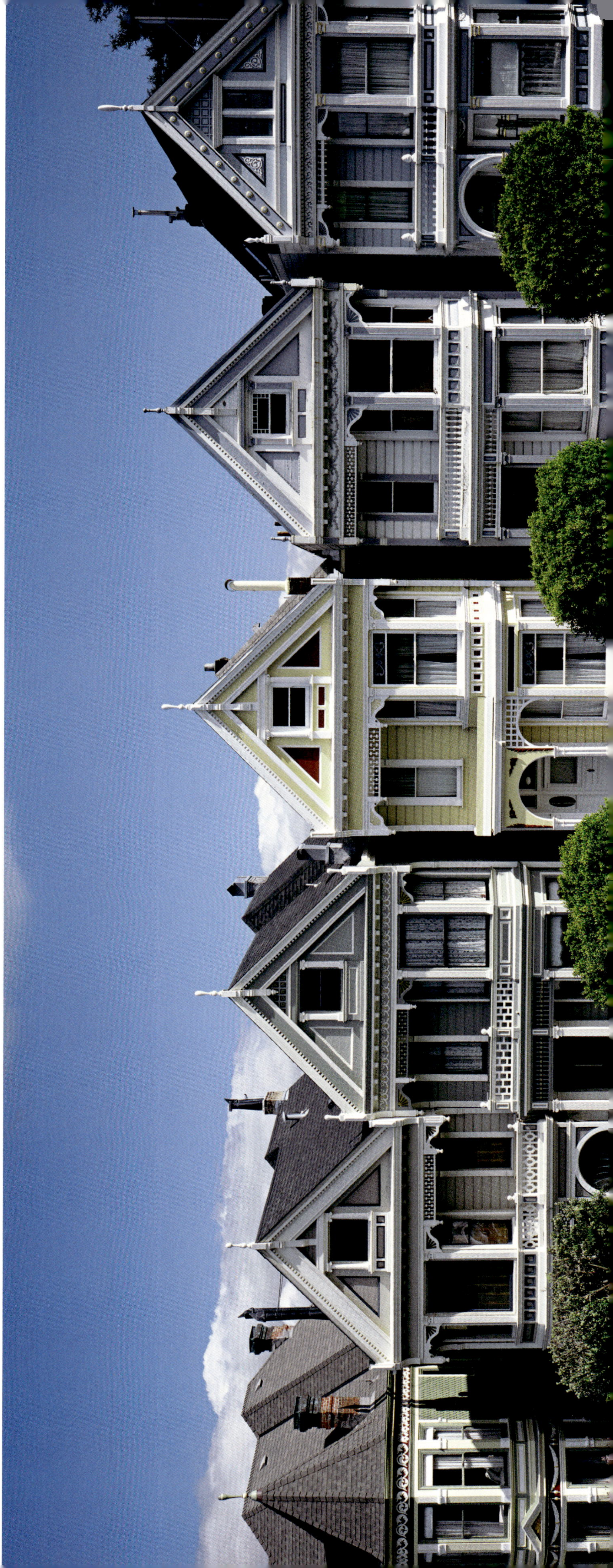

Downtown San Francisco 12

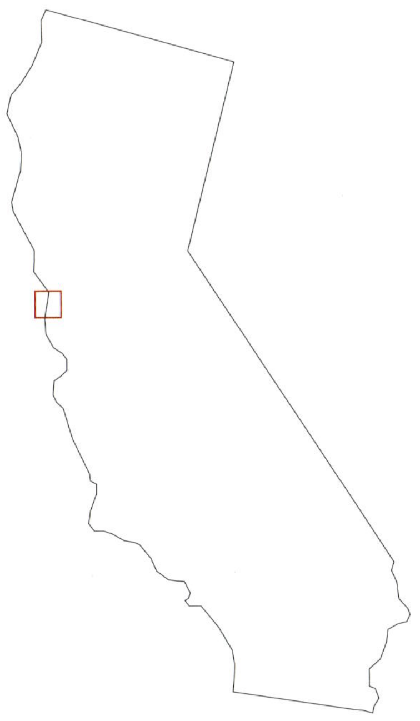

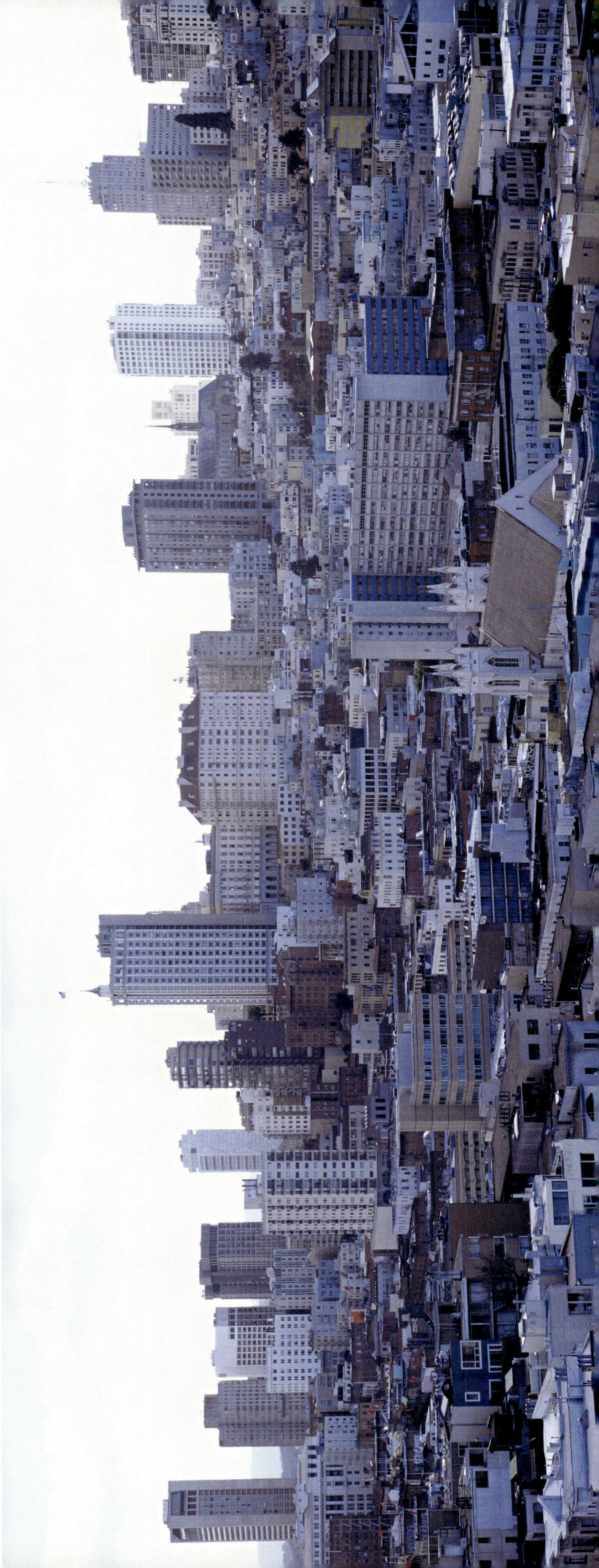

Death Valley National Park 13

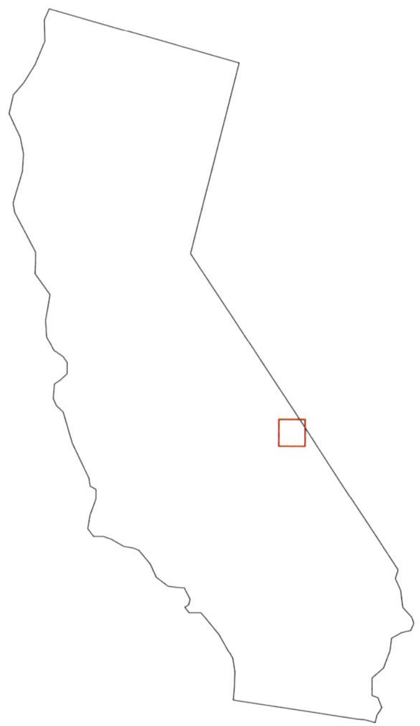

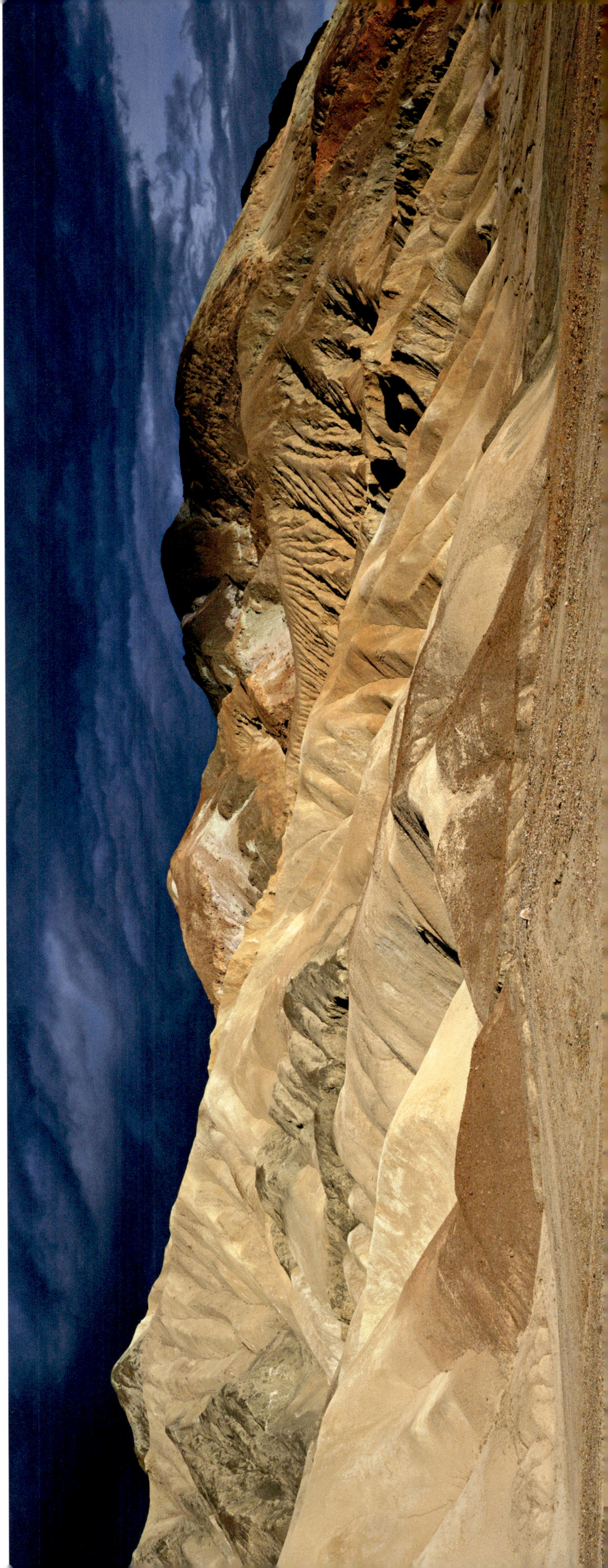

Mesquite Flat Sand Dunes, Death Valley National Park   14

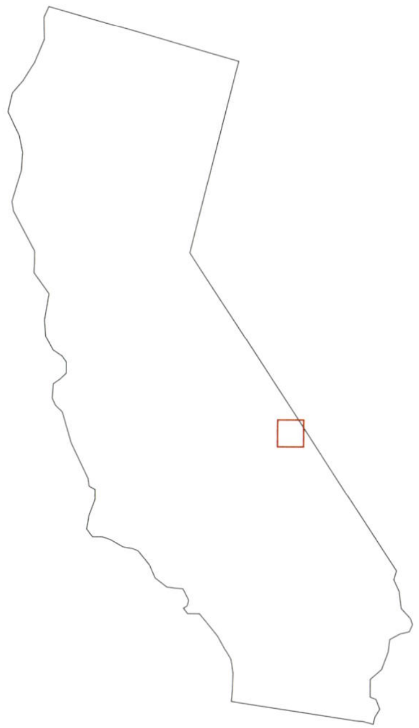

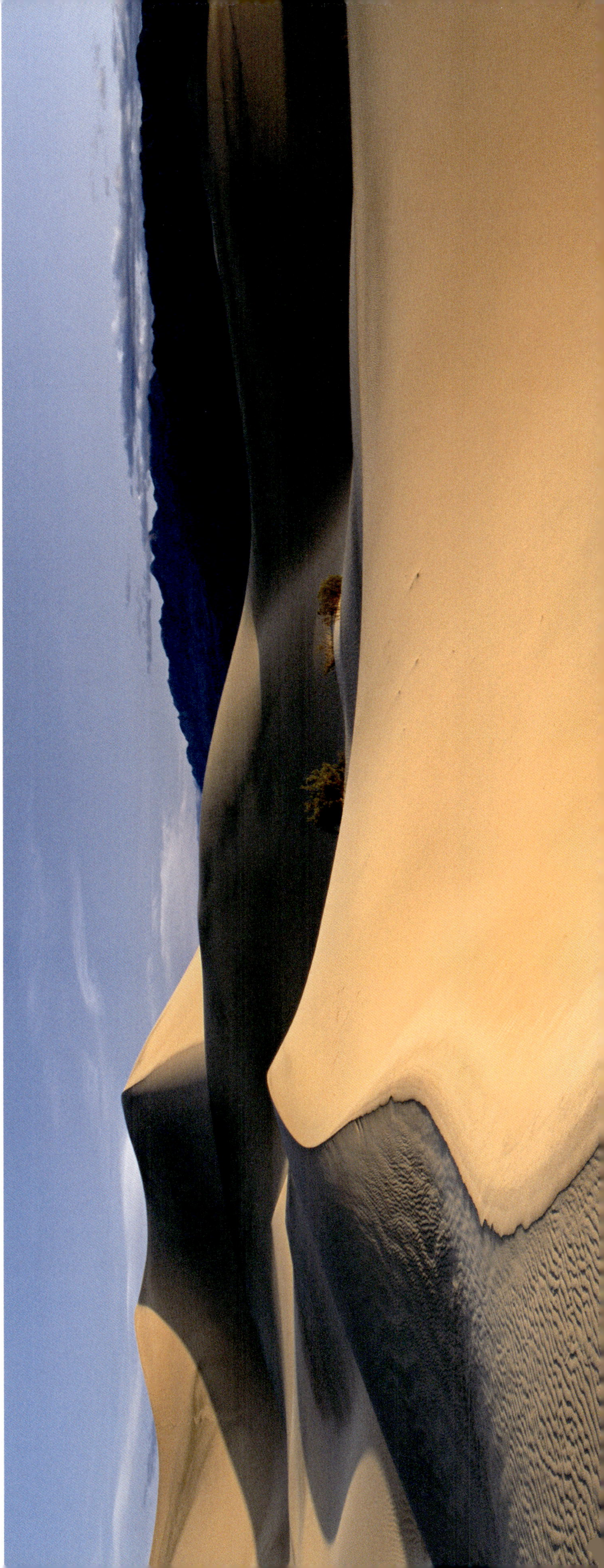

Racetrack, Death Valley National Park 15

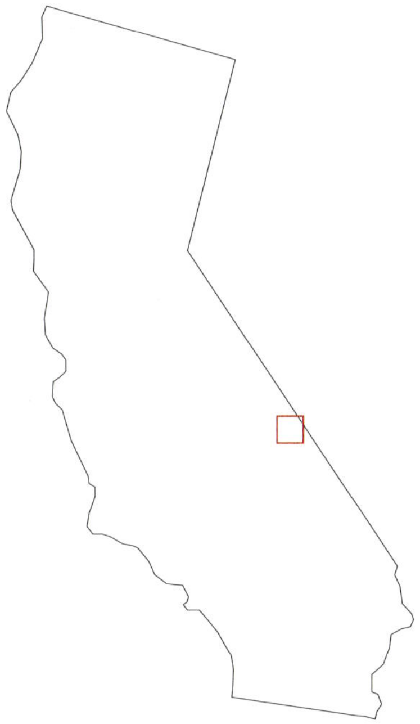

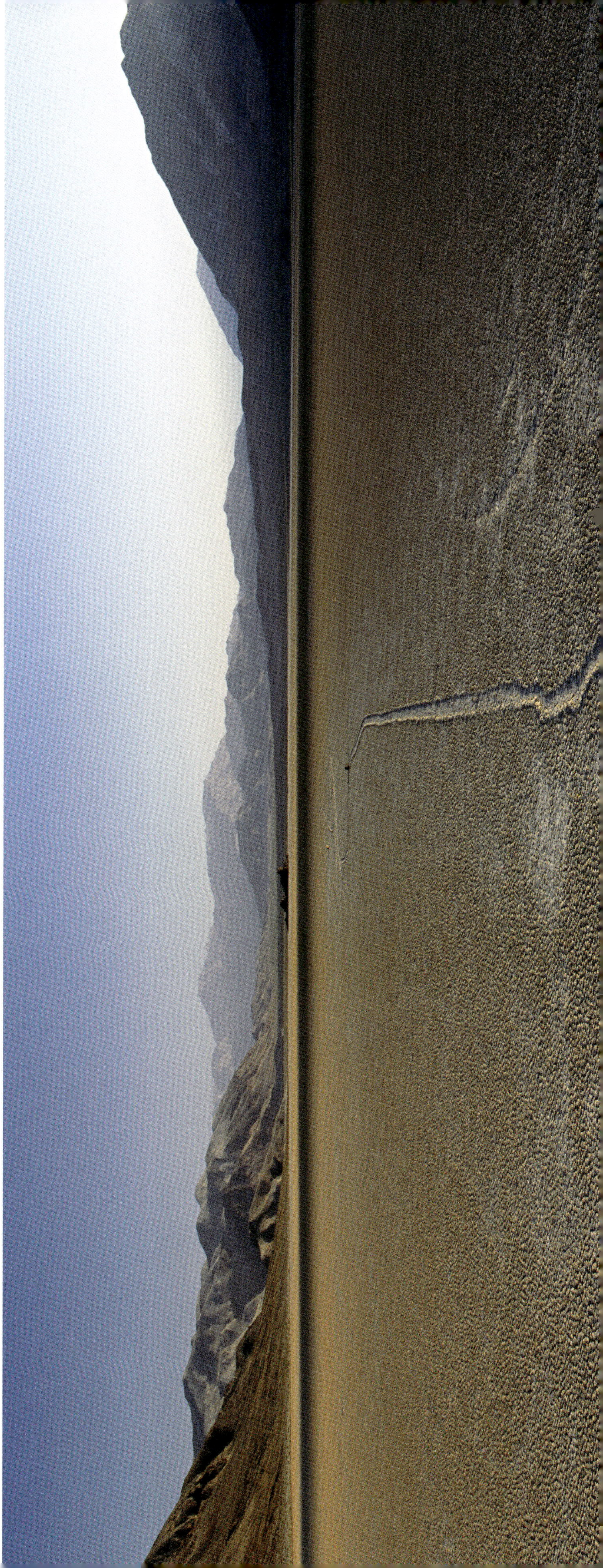

Zabriskie Point, Death Valley National Park 16

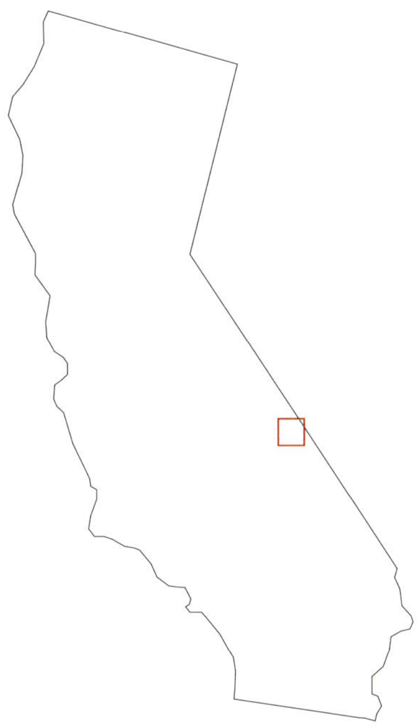

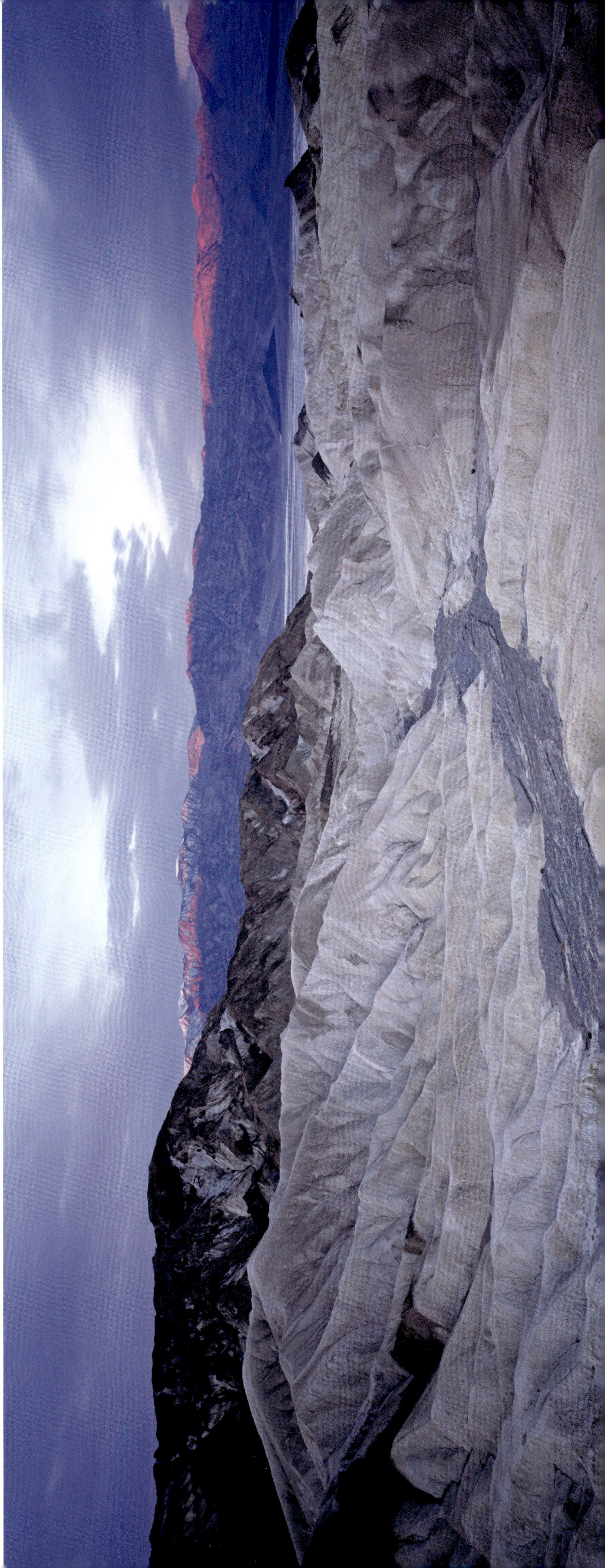

Salvation Mountain, Salton Sea 17

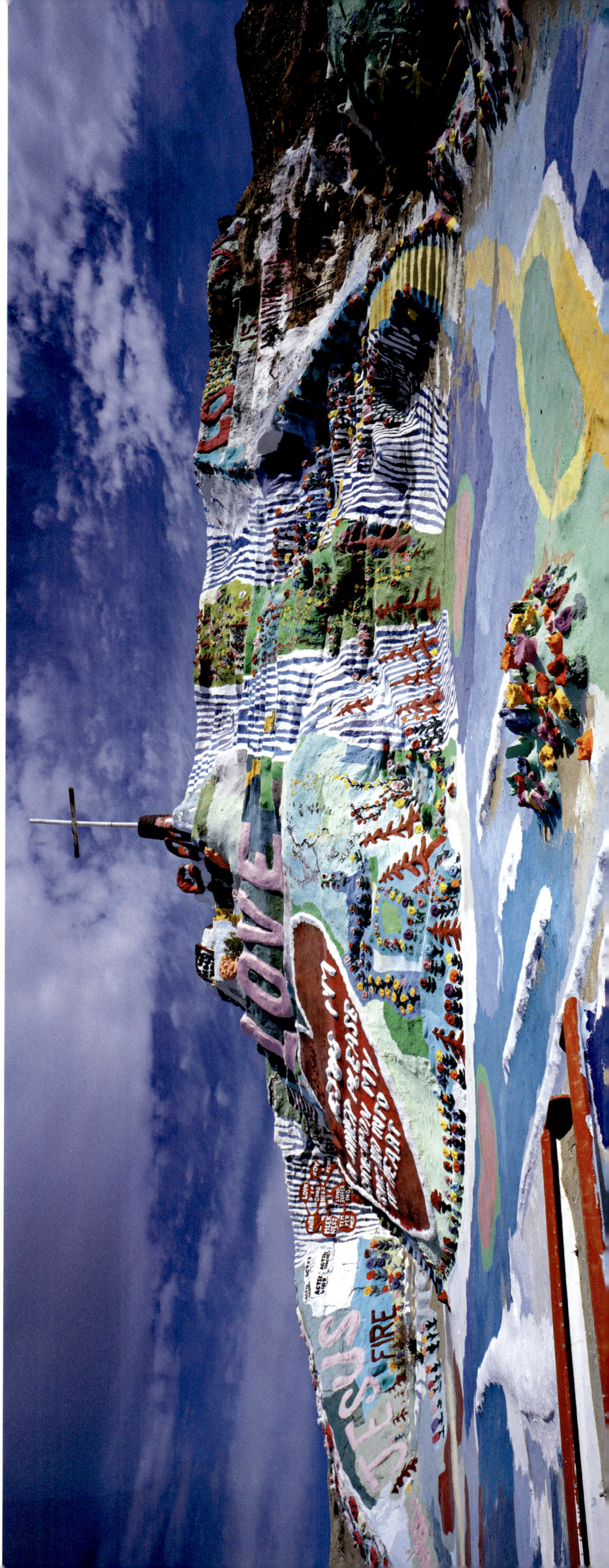
LOVE
JESUS
FIRE

Trailer community Slab City 18

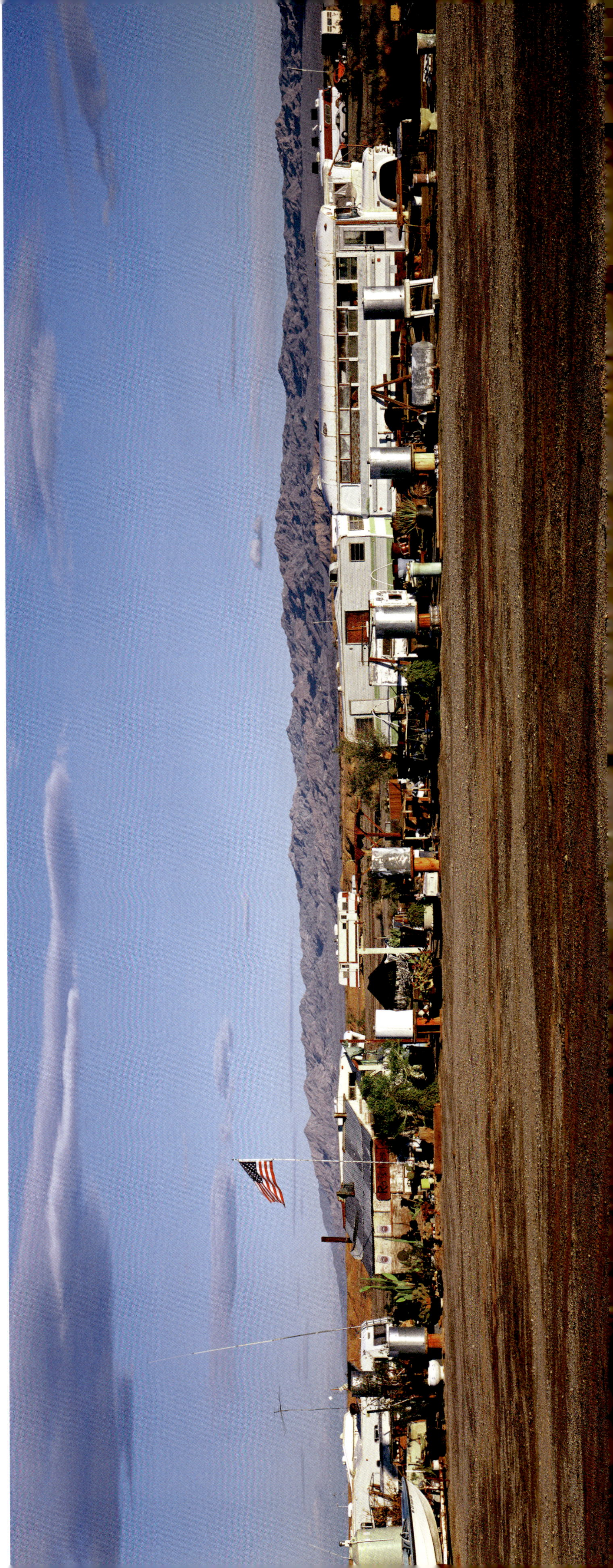

Container train in Mojave Desert   19

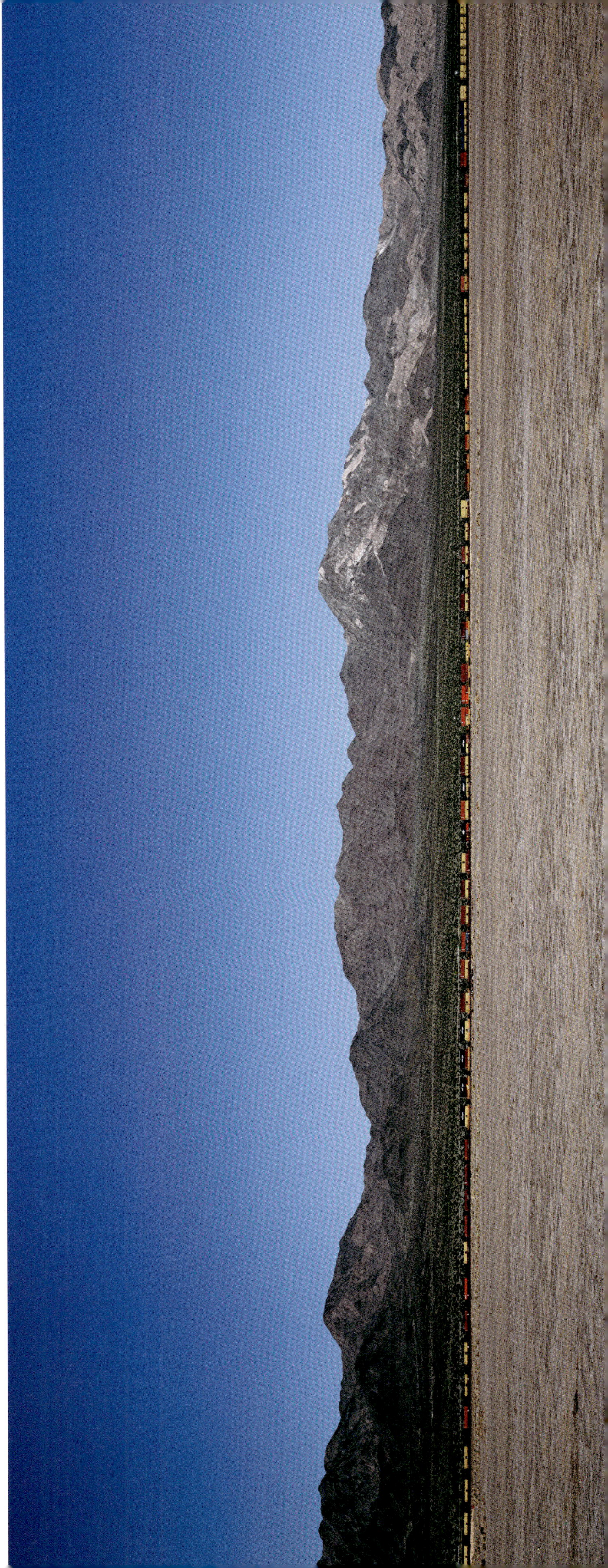

Sunset, Lake Tahoe   20

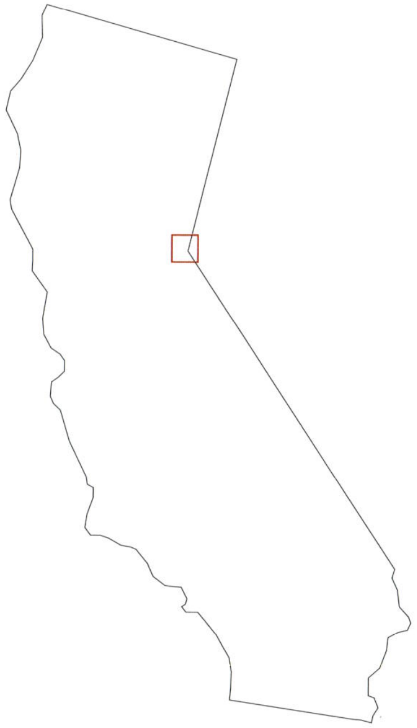

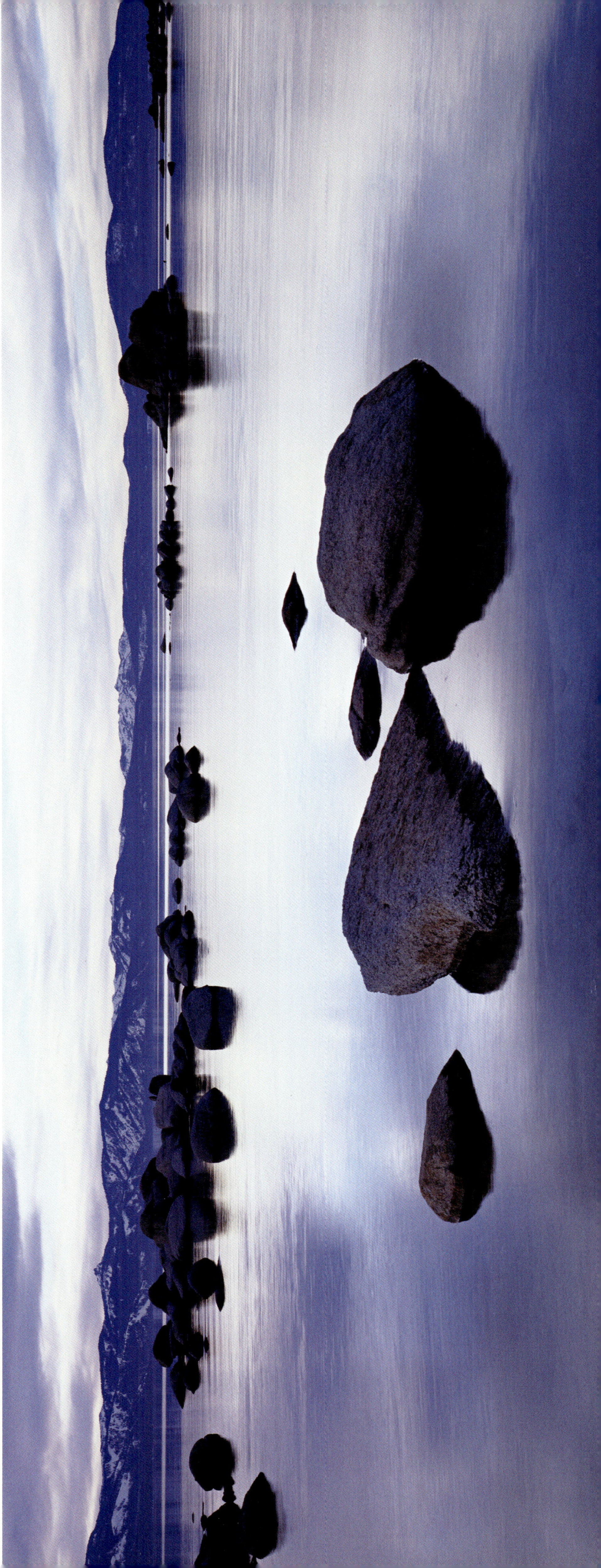

Emerald Bay, Lake Tahoe 21

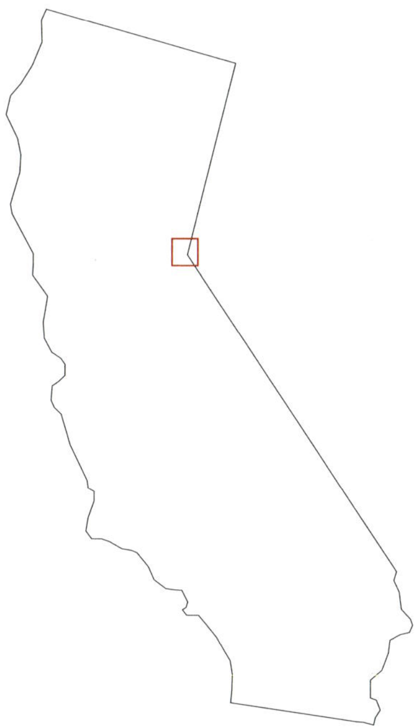

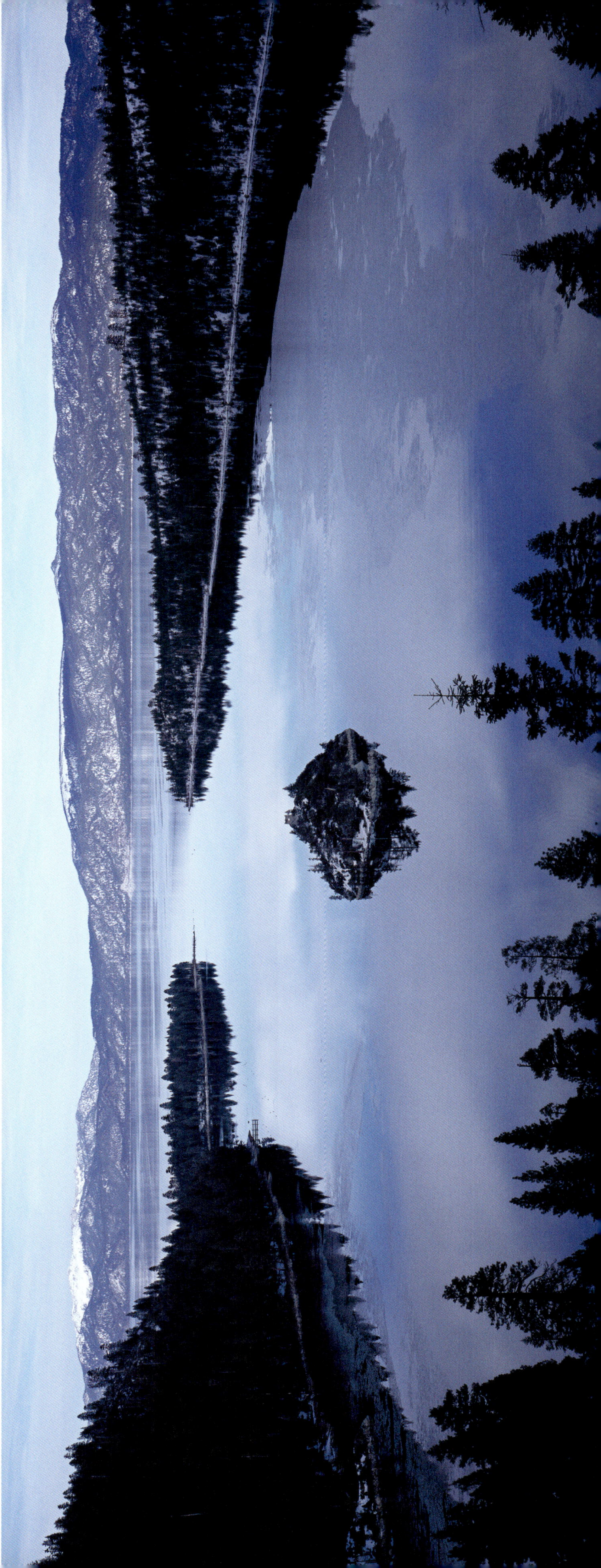

Sunrise near Bishop 22

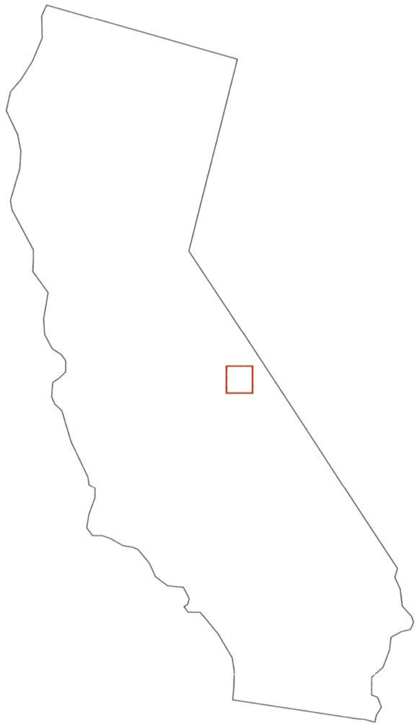

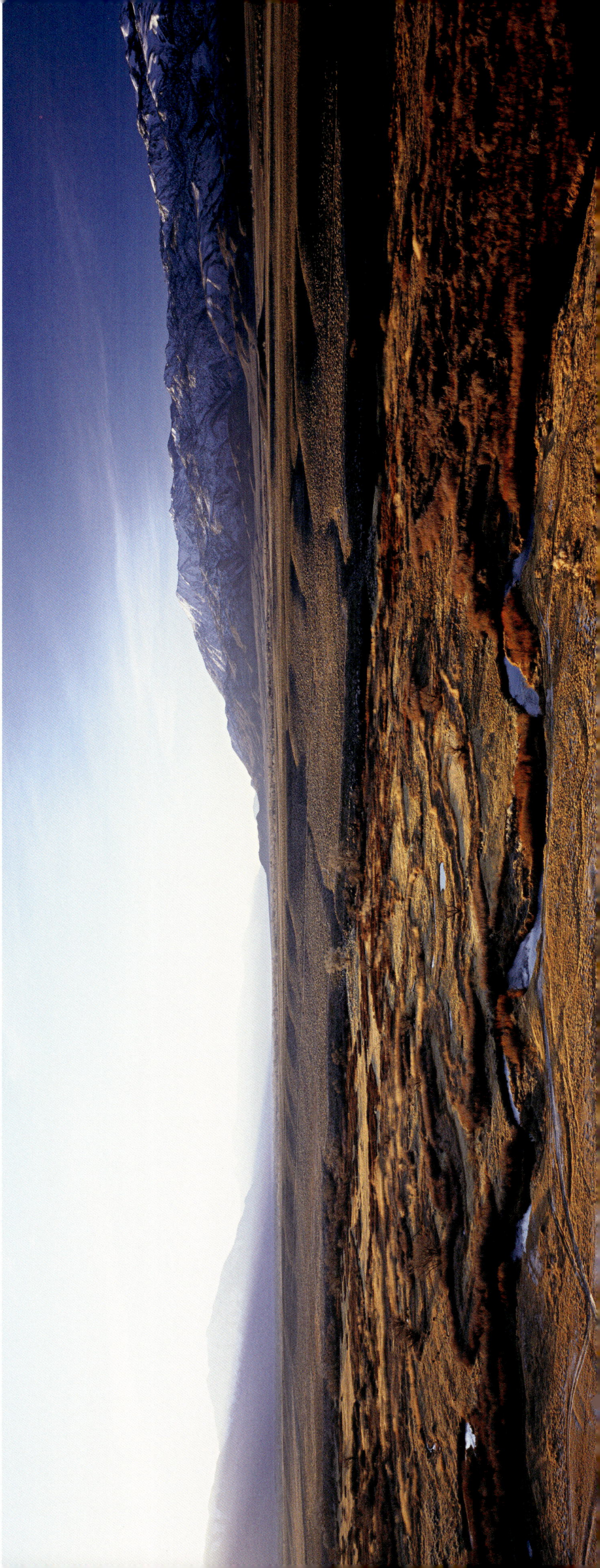

Alabama Hills 23

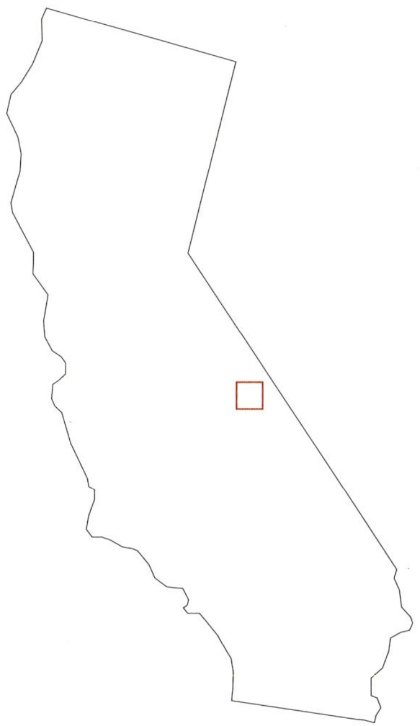

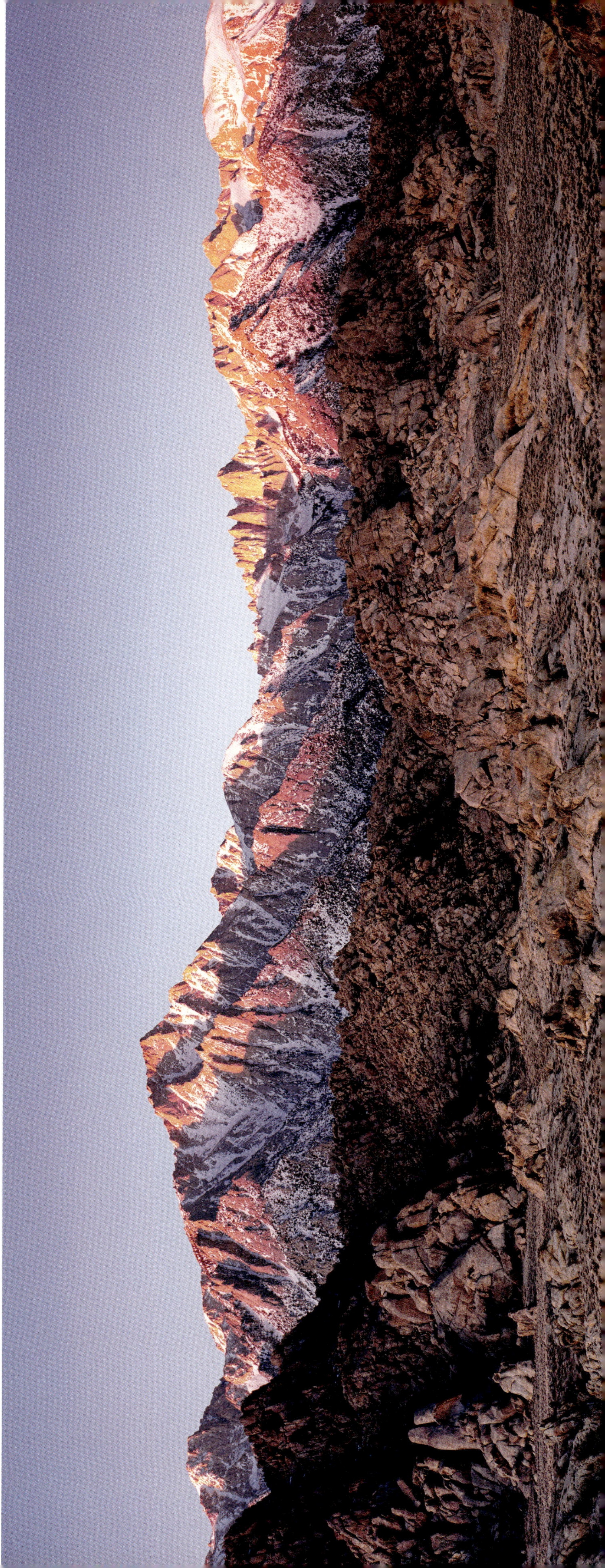

Lake near Lone Pine   24

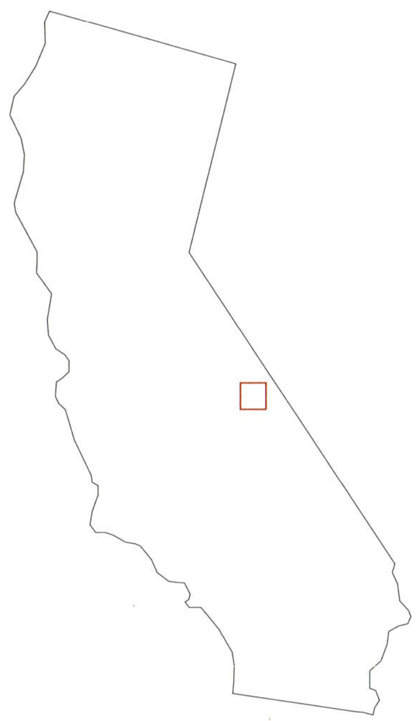

Yosemite National Park 25

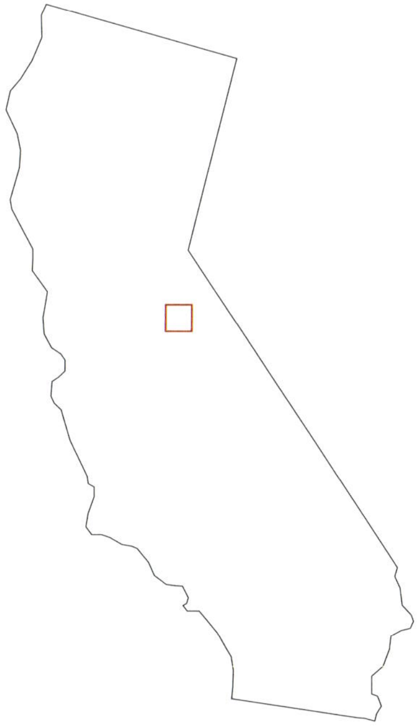

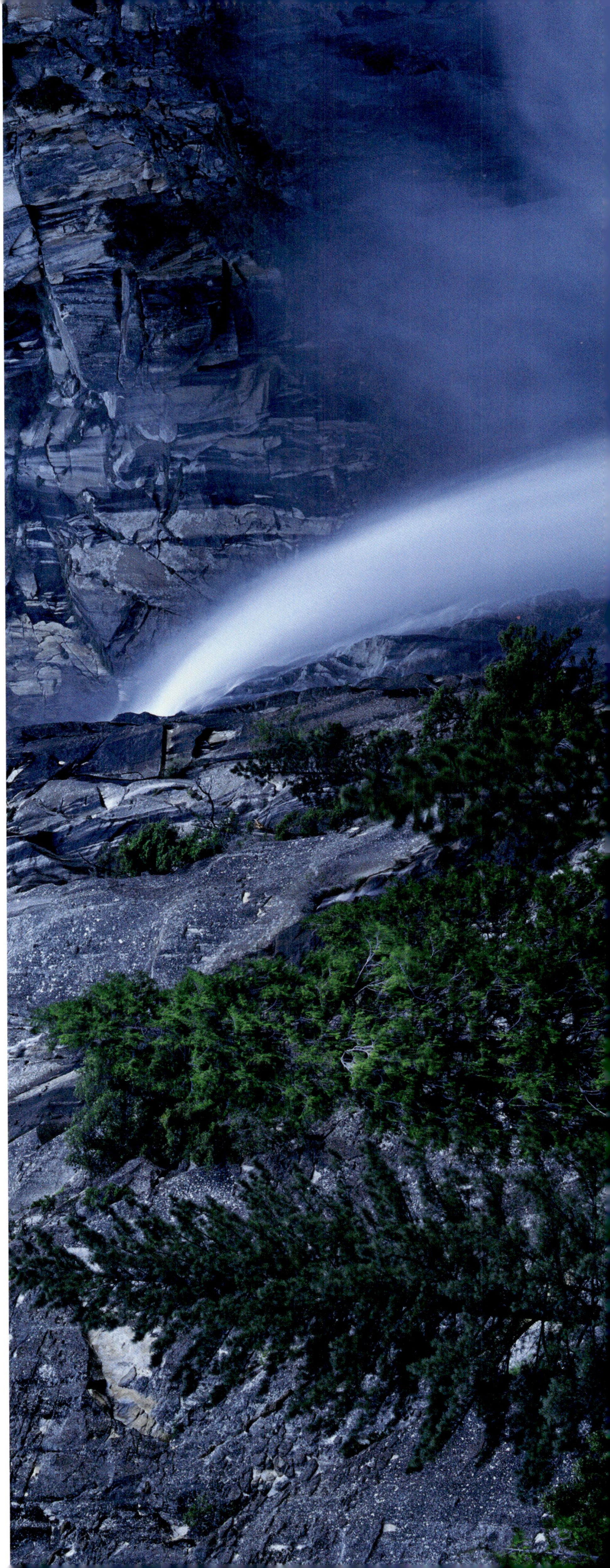

McArthur Burney Falls Memorial State Park 26

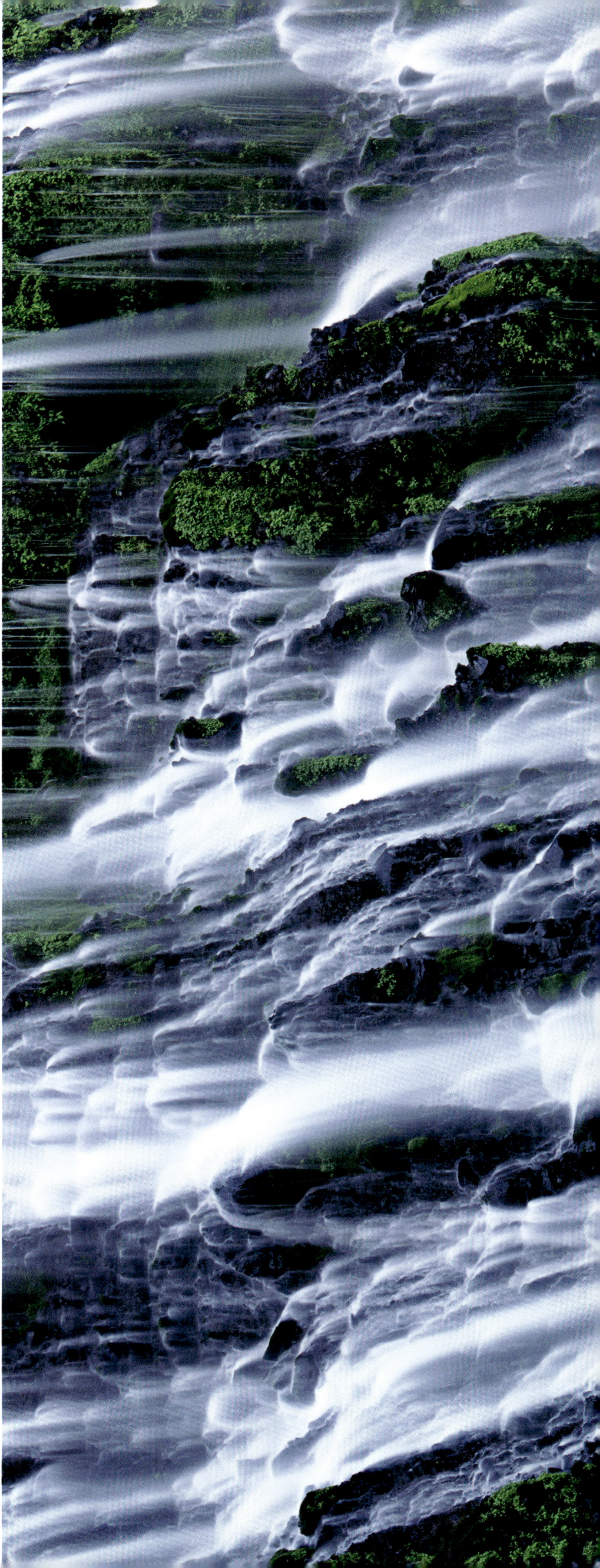

Anza Borrego Desert State Park 27

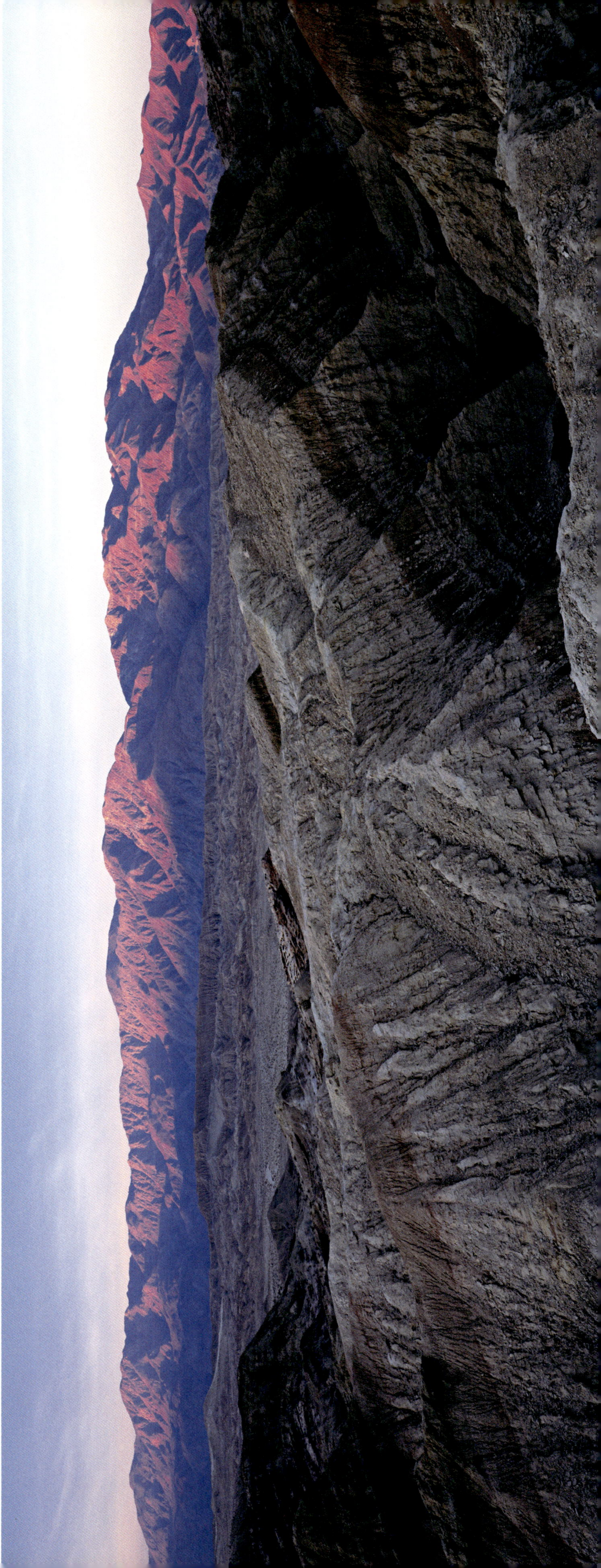

Joshua Tree National Park   28

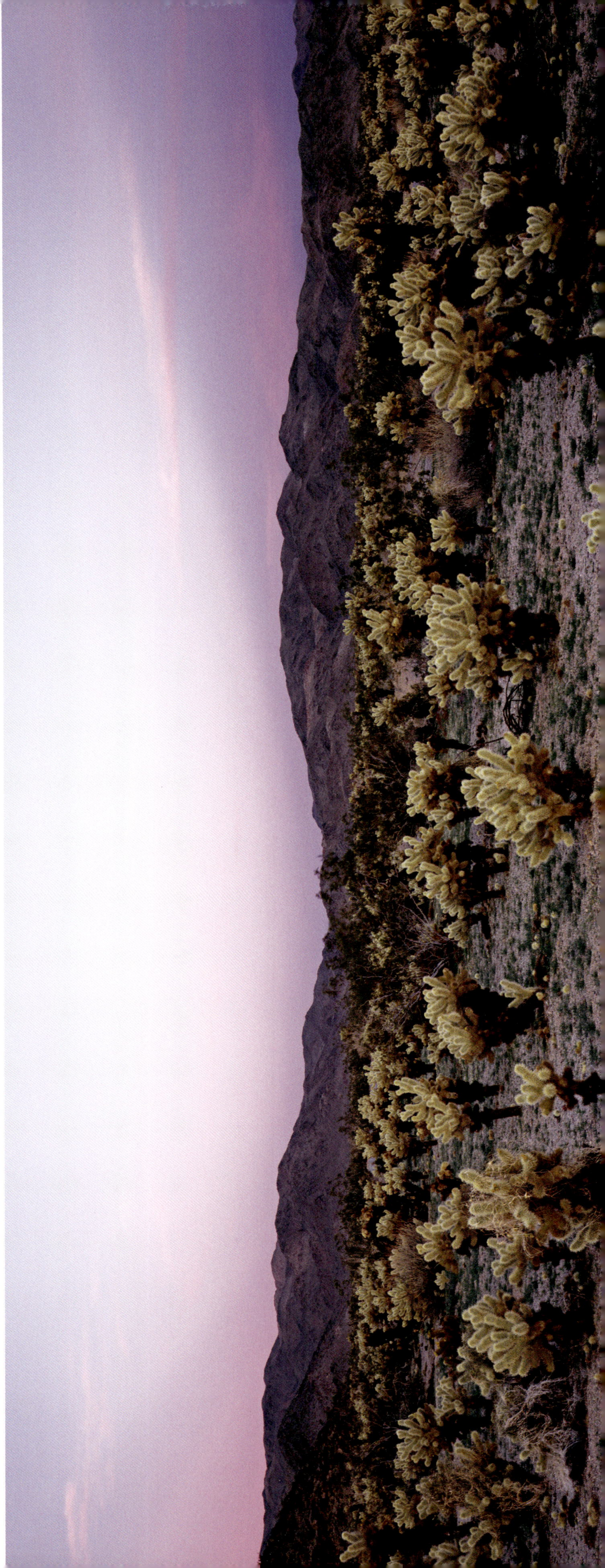

Joshua Tree National Park 29

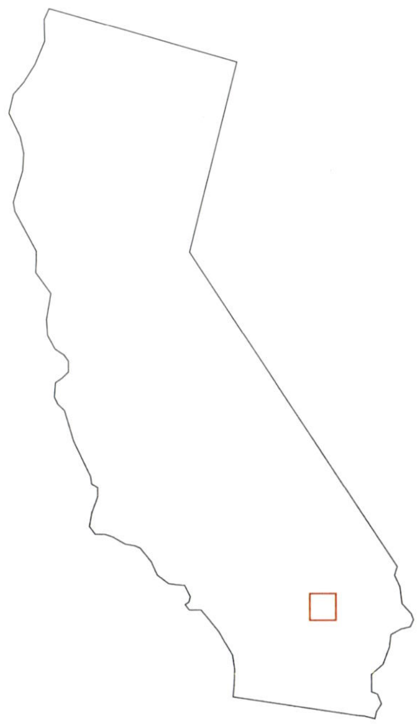

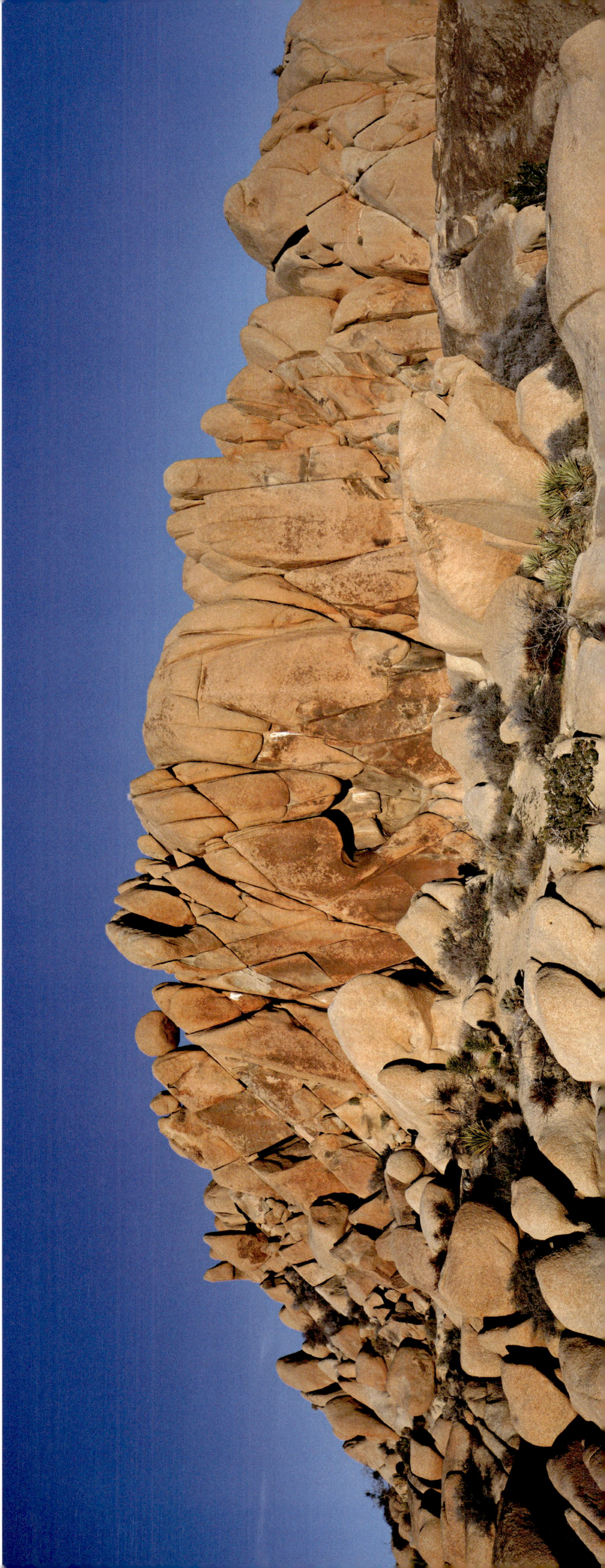

Joshua Tree National Park 30

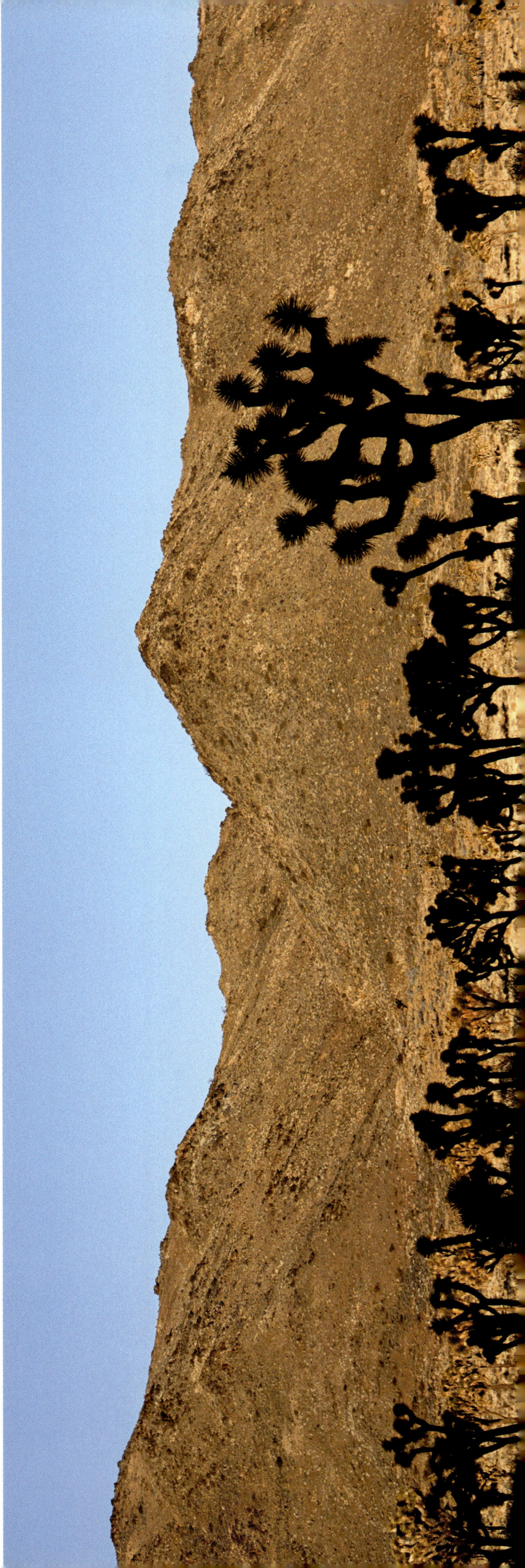

Horton Plaza, Gaslamp Quarter, San Diego

GREAT KHAN'S
GREAT KHAN
currito
BURRITOS
WITHOUT BORDERS
NORDSTROM
Health care
A WHOLE NEW WAY
Westfield
Fire Hose

Mural in San Diego 32

History Of Our Community

is
information on the past
& the lives of its
past & present
residents & leaves its
legacy future generations

Coronado Bridge, San Diego   33

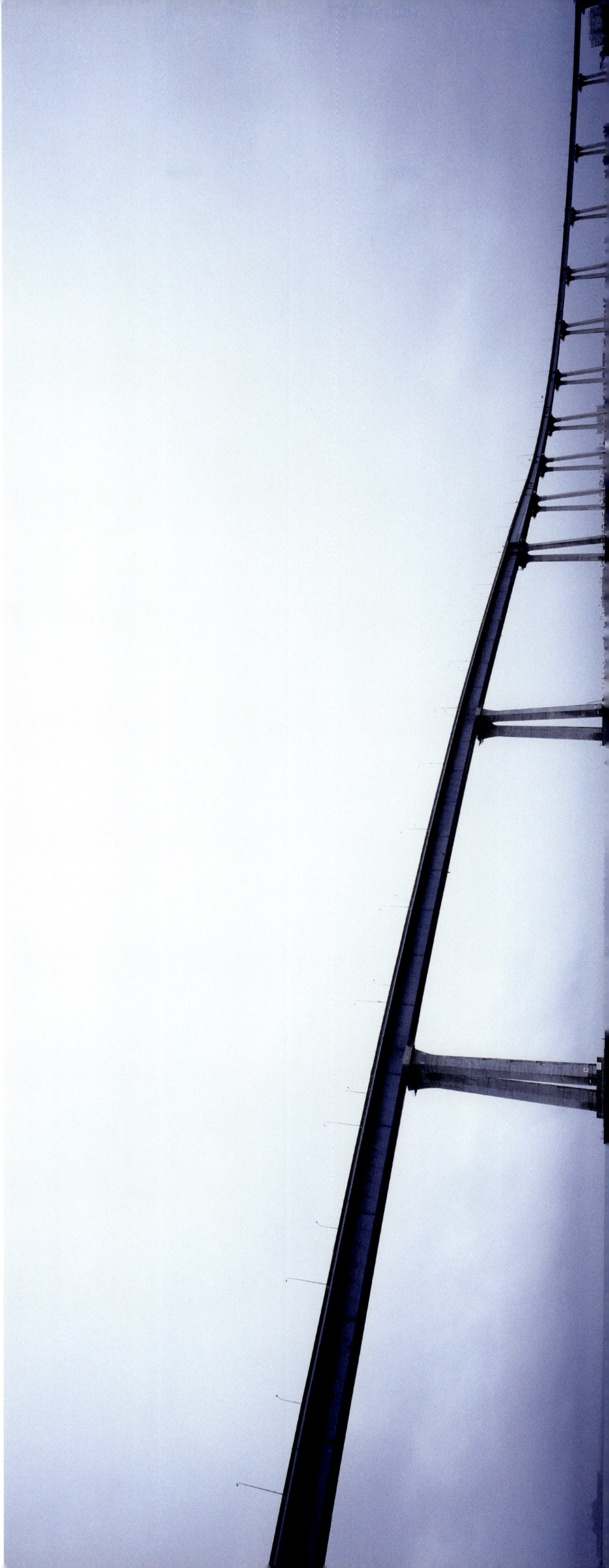

California State Capitol, Sacramento   34

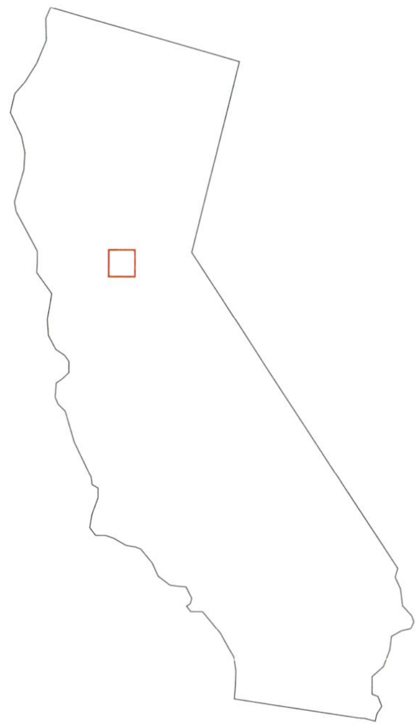

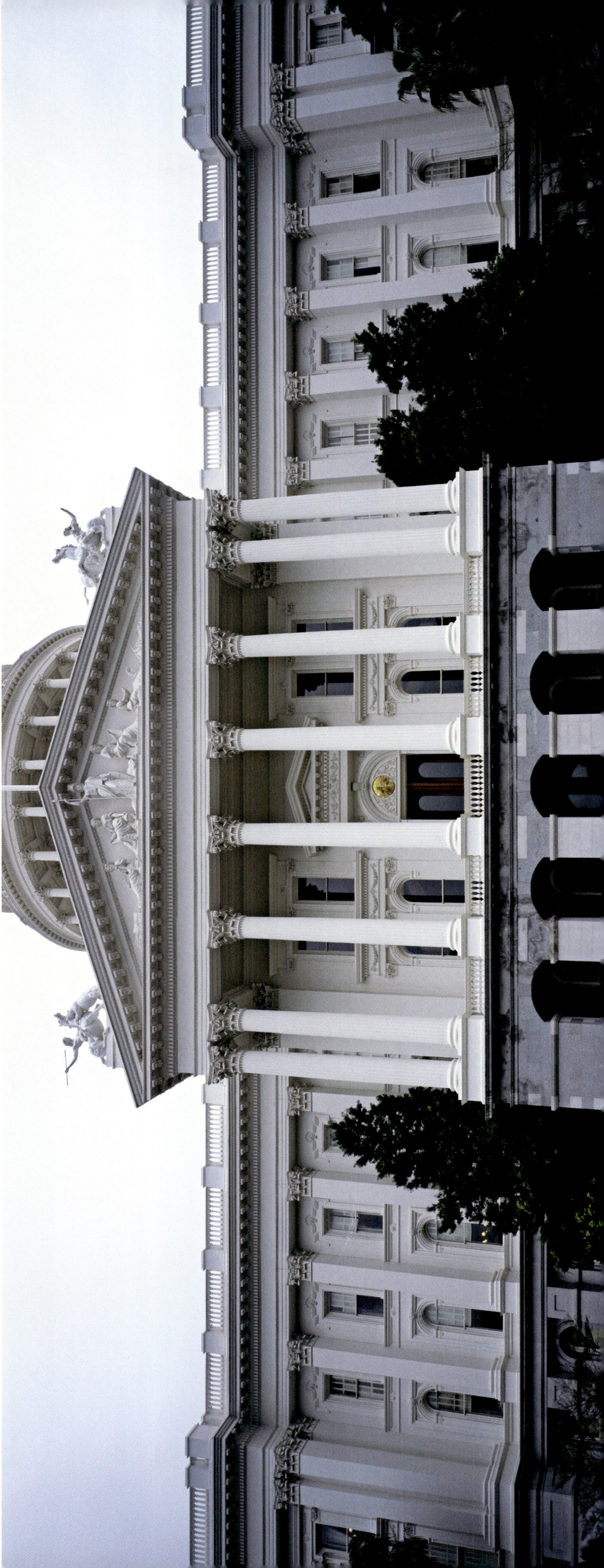

Mission in San Miguel 35

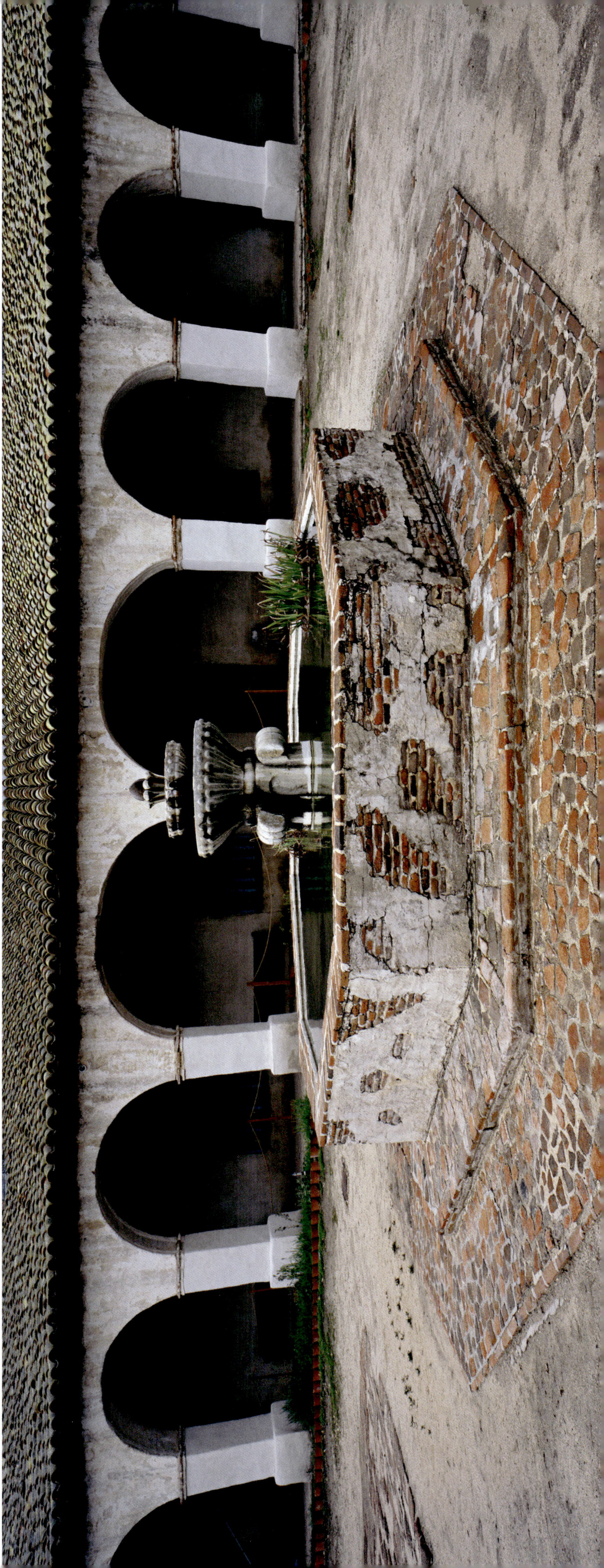

near Baker 36

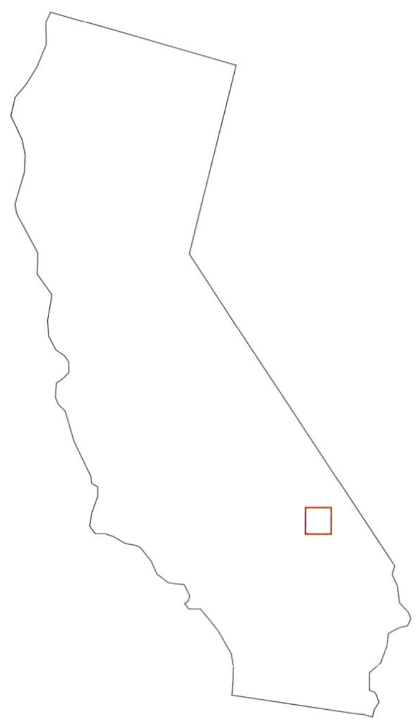

Bob's Big Boy
BREAKFAST BUFFET
BAKER 20 Min

ZZyZx Road near Baker 37

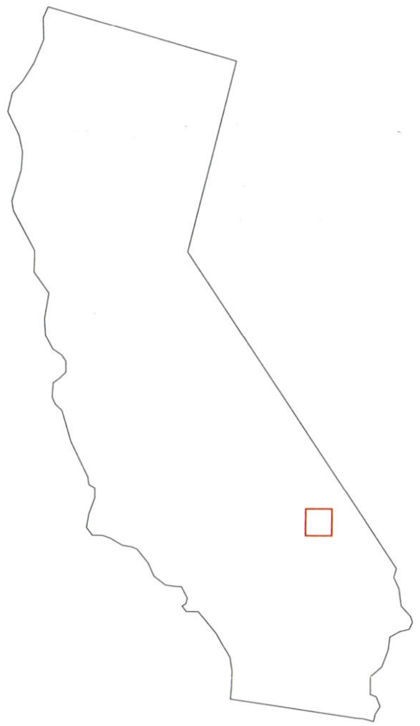

Zzyzx Rd

Salton Sea   38

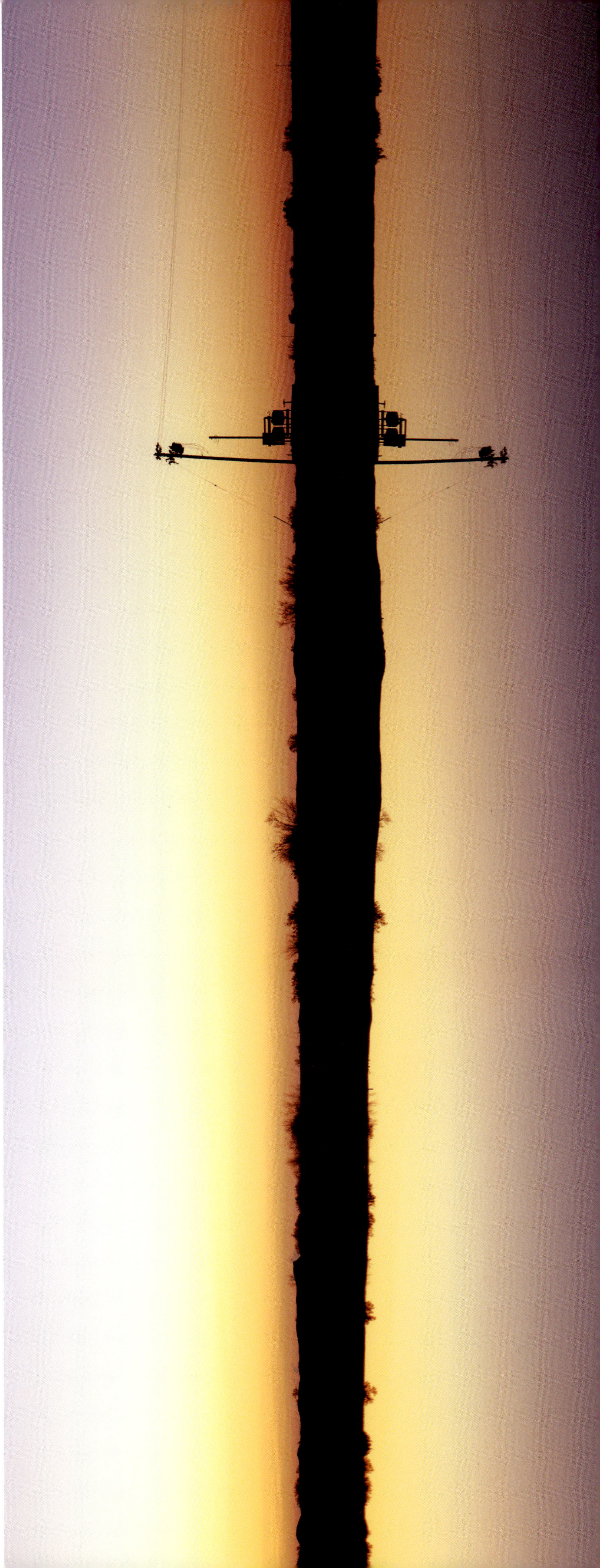

Salt Point State Park   39

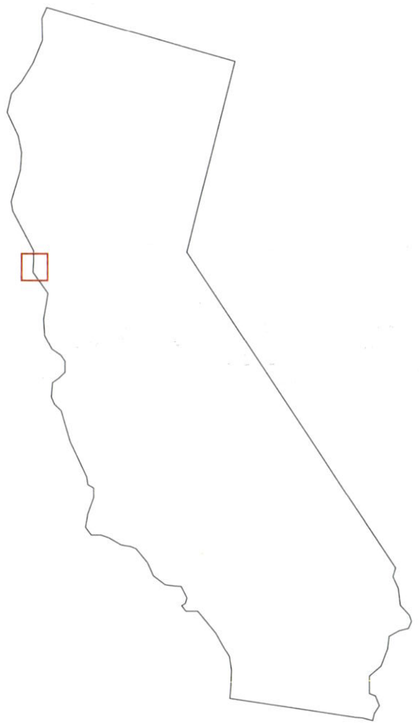

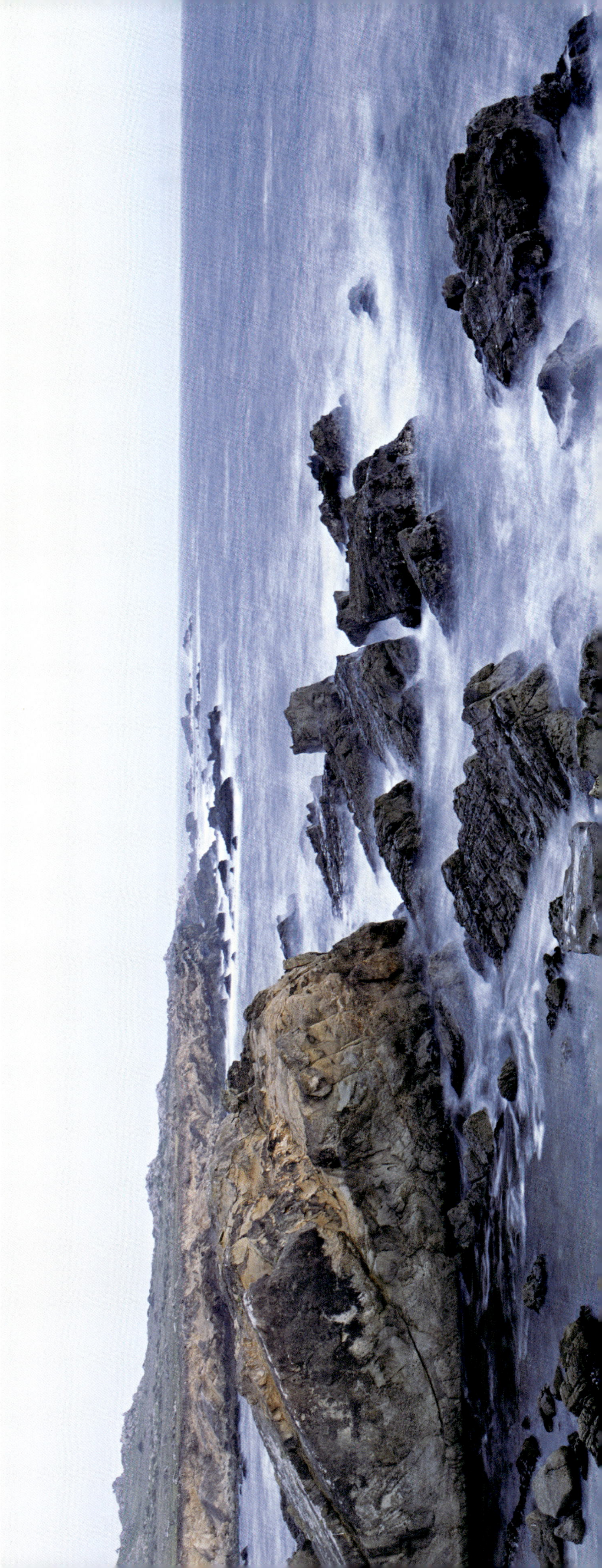

Salt Point State Park   40

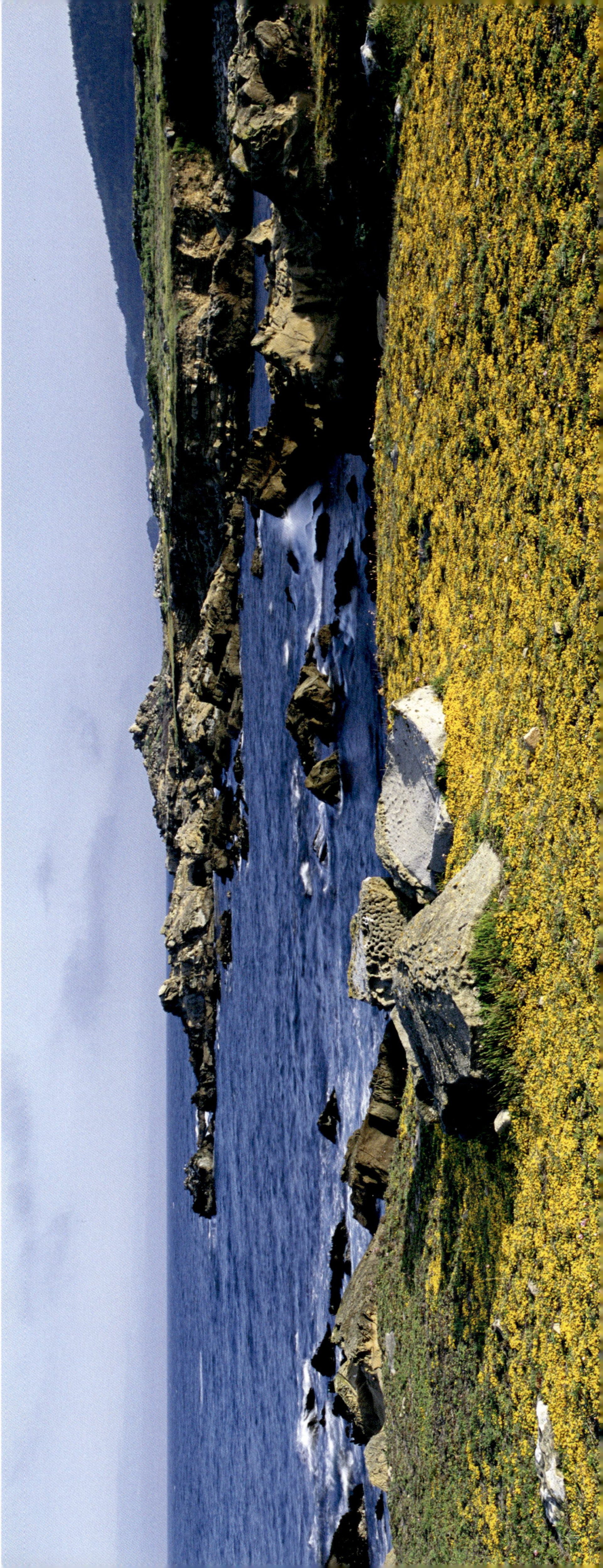

Sonoma Coast 41

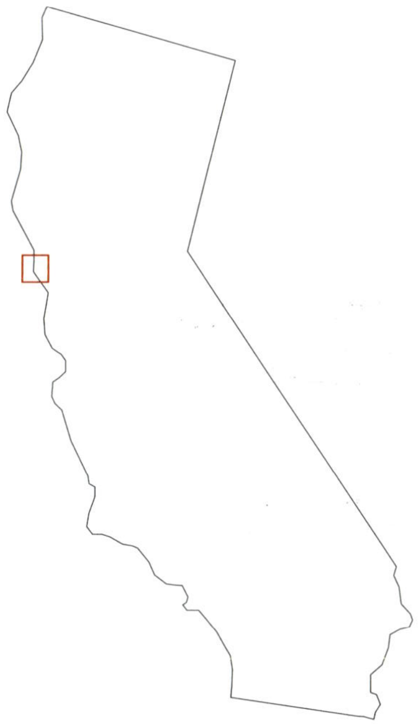

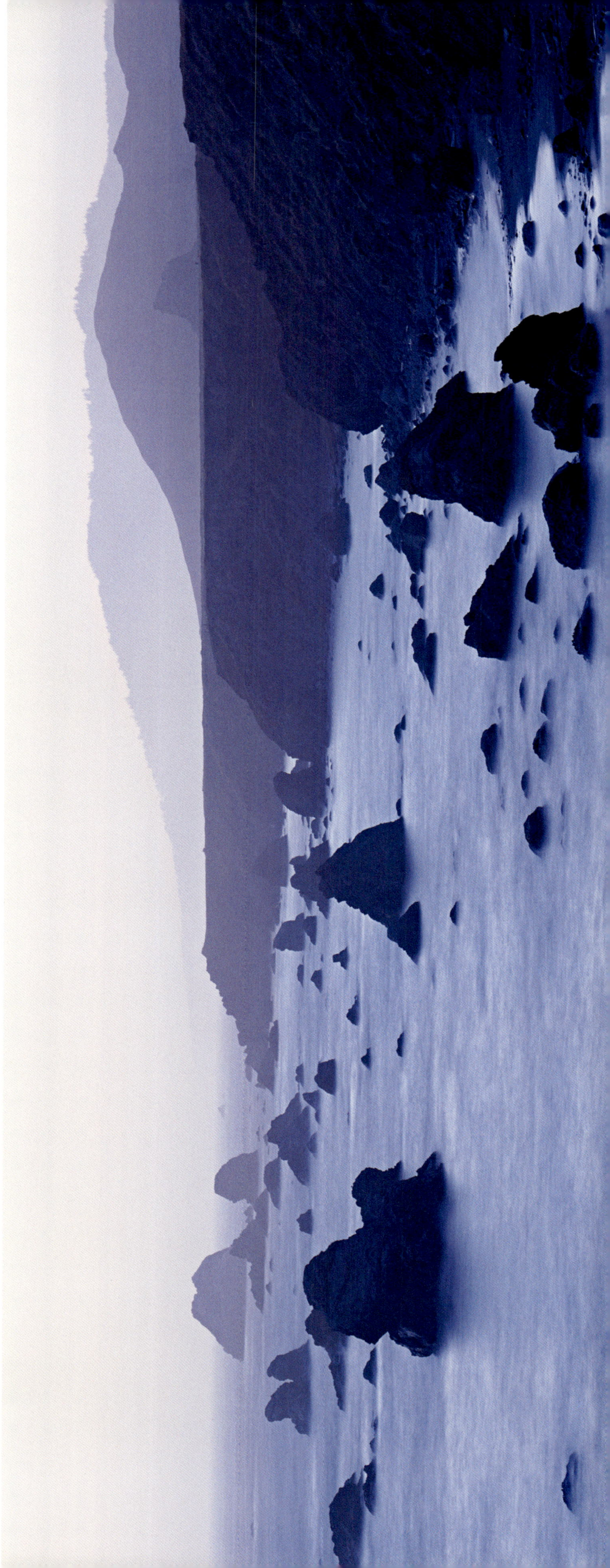

Mt. Shasta 42

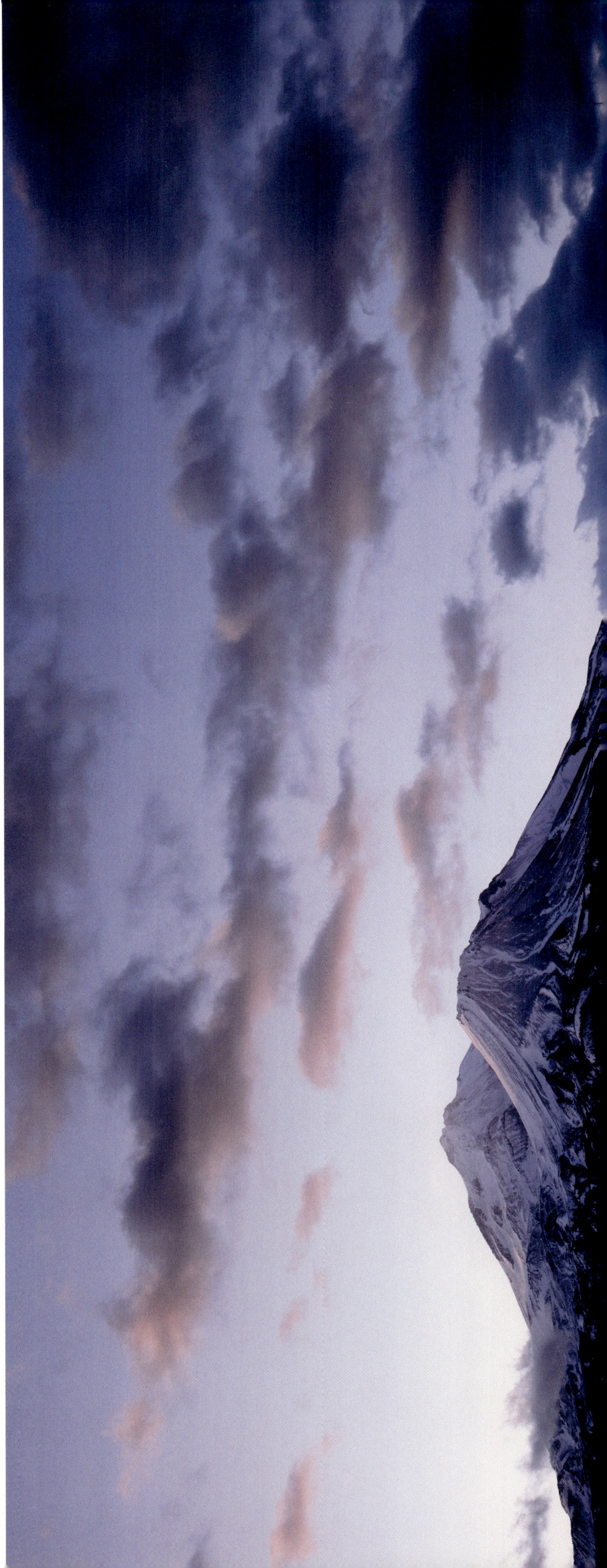

Windmills near Palm Springs 43

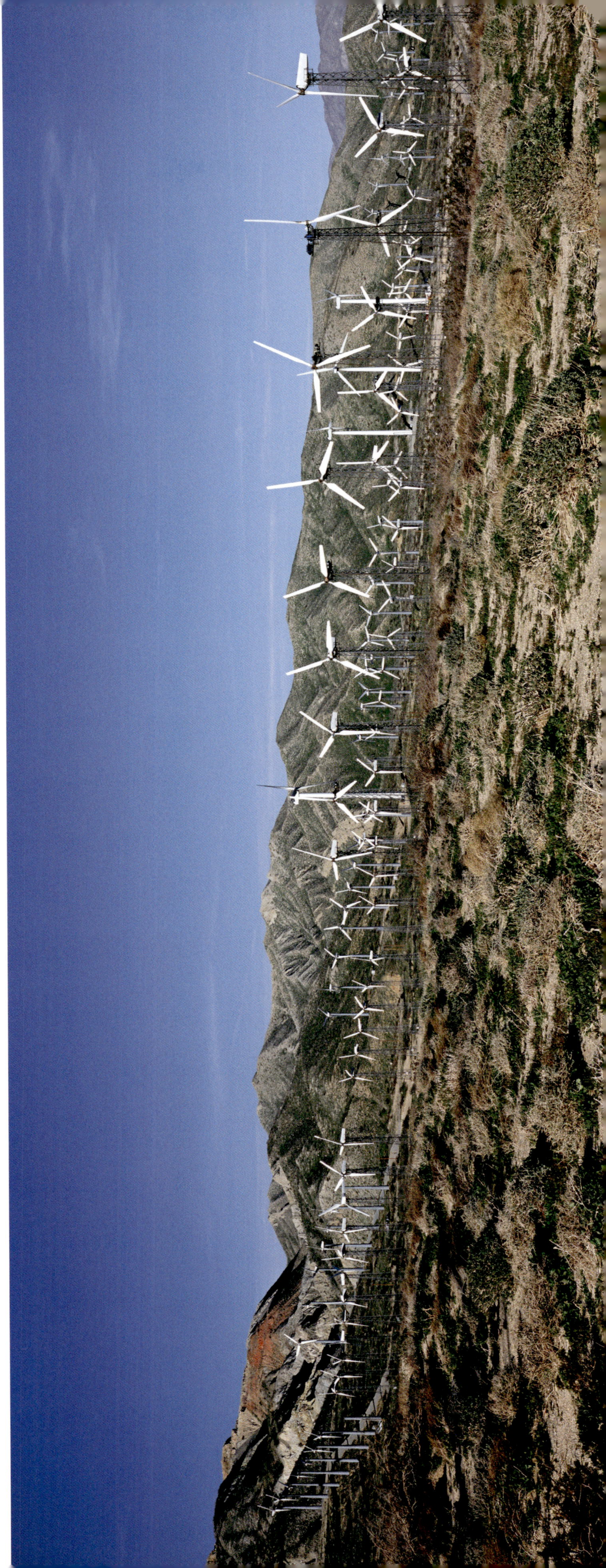

Palm trees in Palm Springs 44

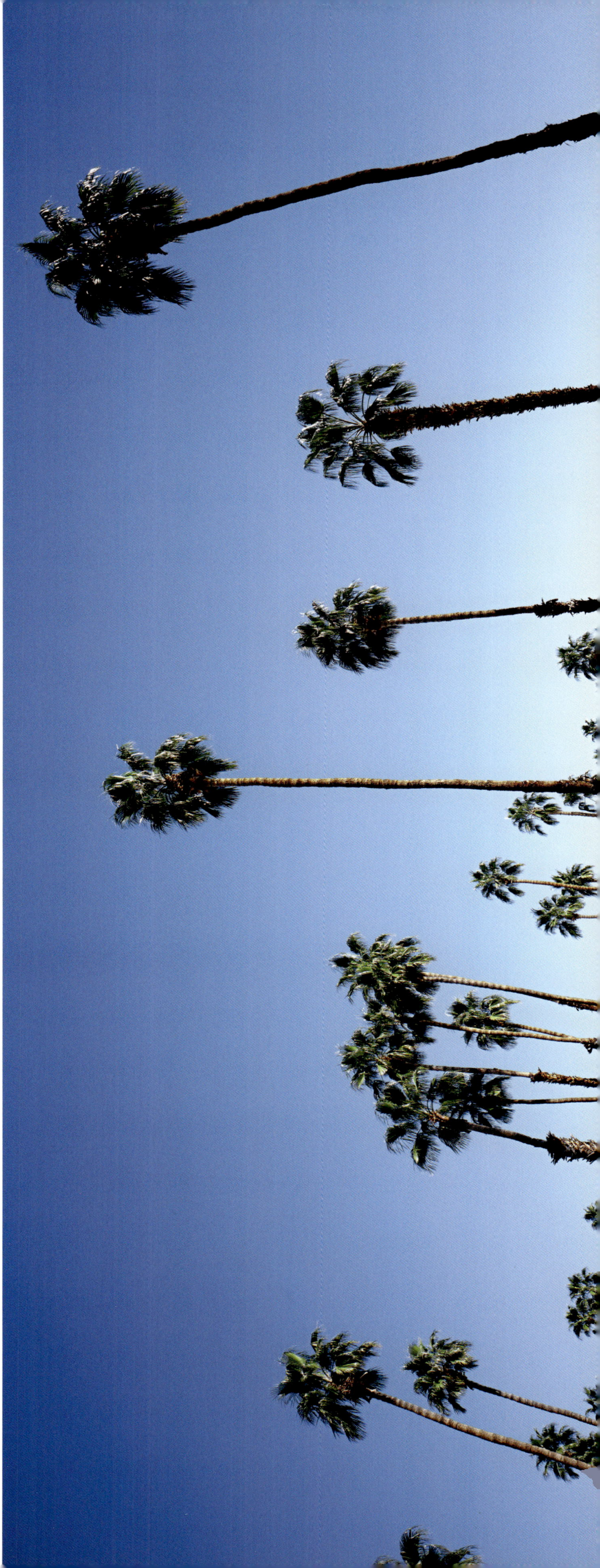

Jellyfish at Monterey Bay Aquarium 45

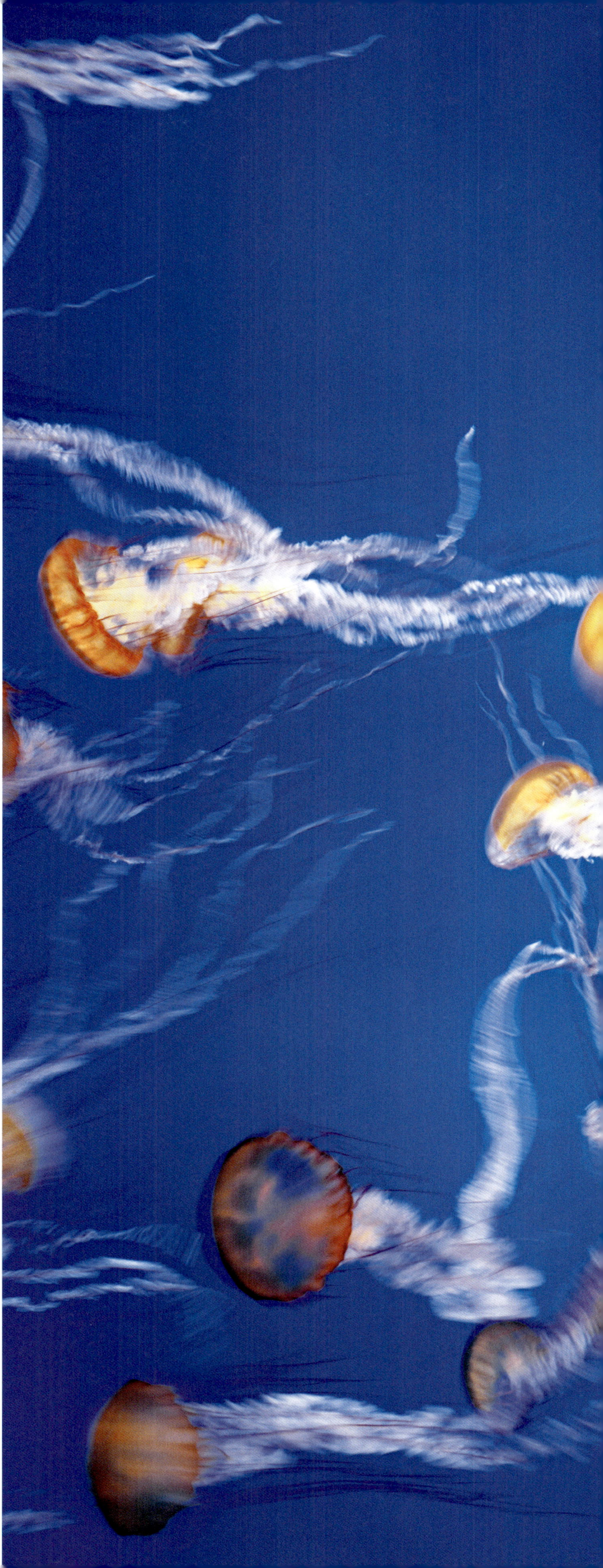

Horseback riders on the beach of Crescent City 46

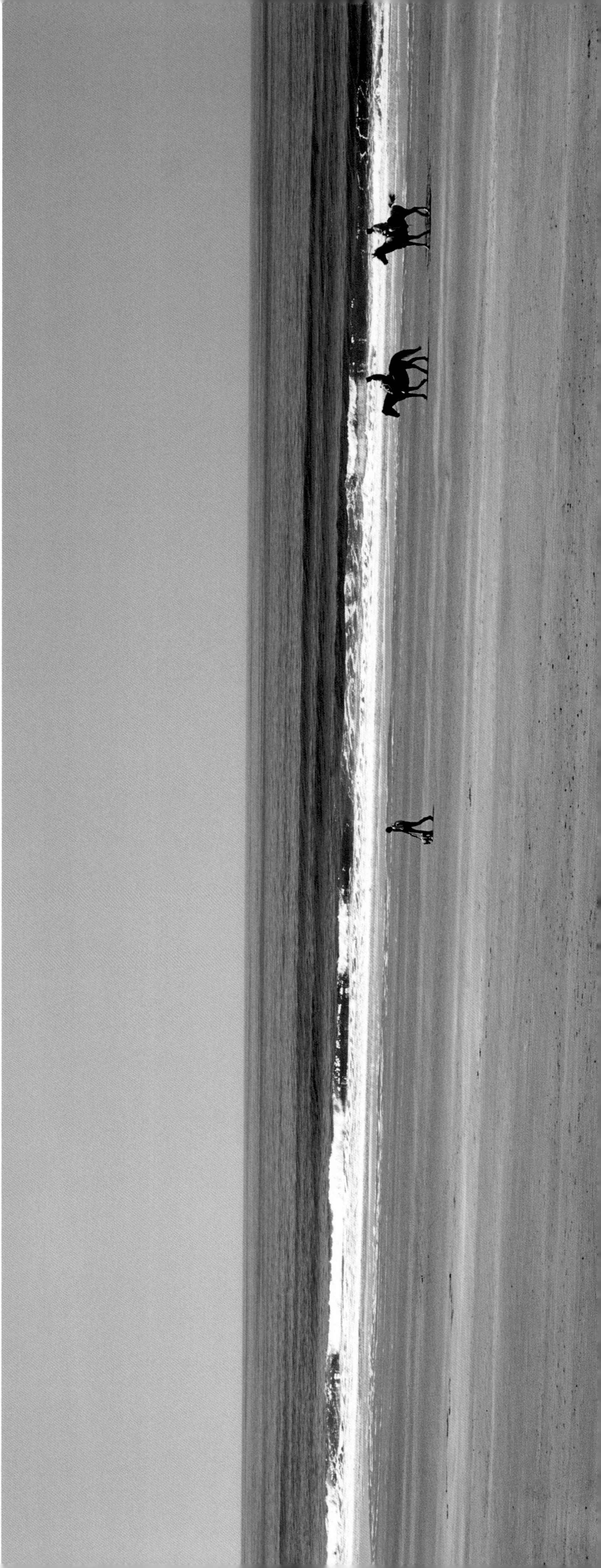

Windsurfers off Sonoma Coast   47

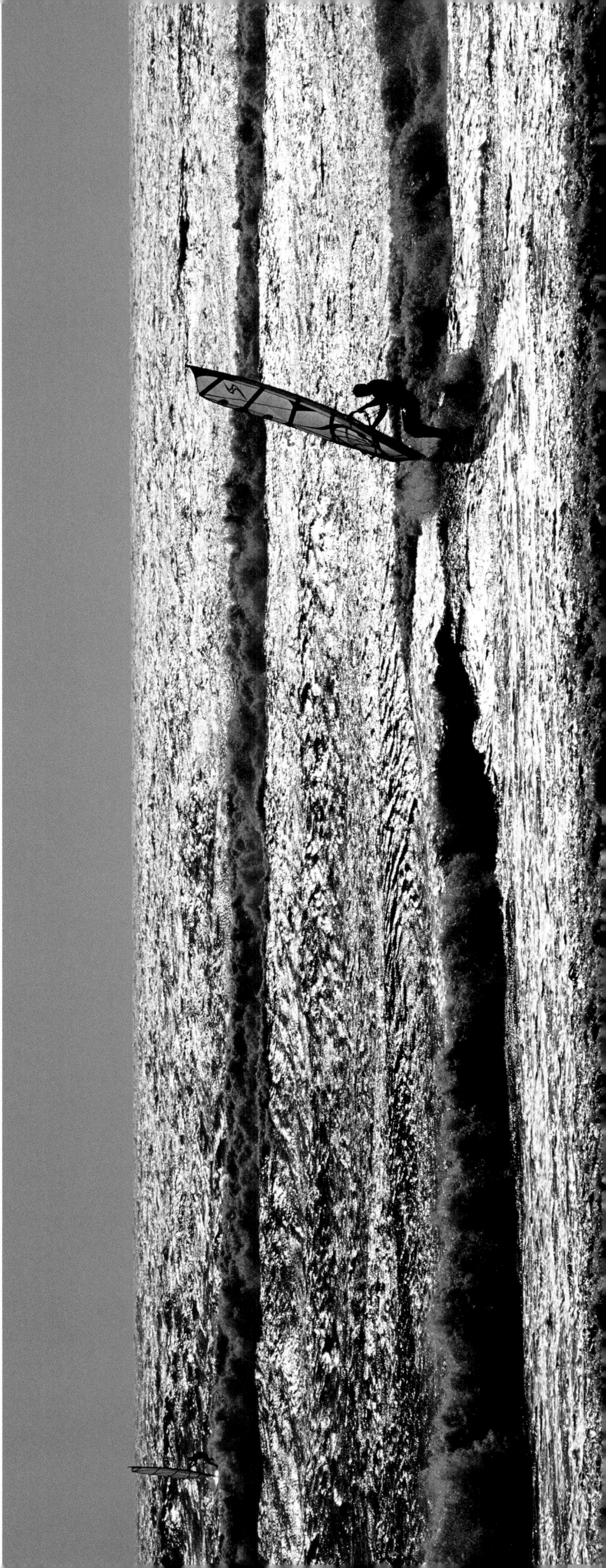

Poppy field, Tehachapi Mountains 48

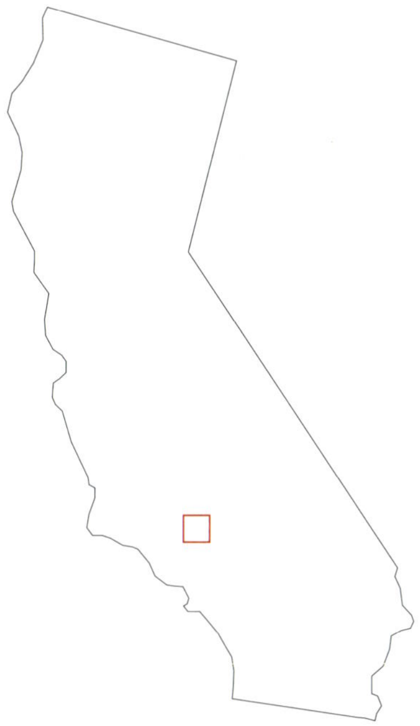

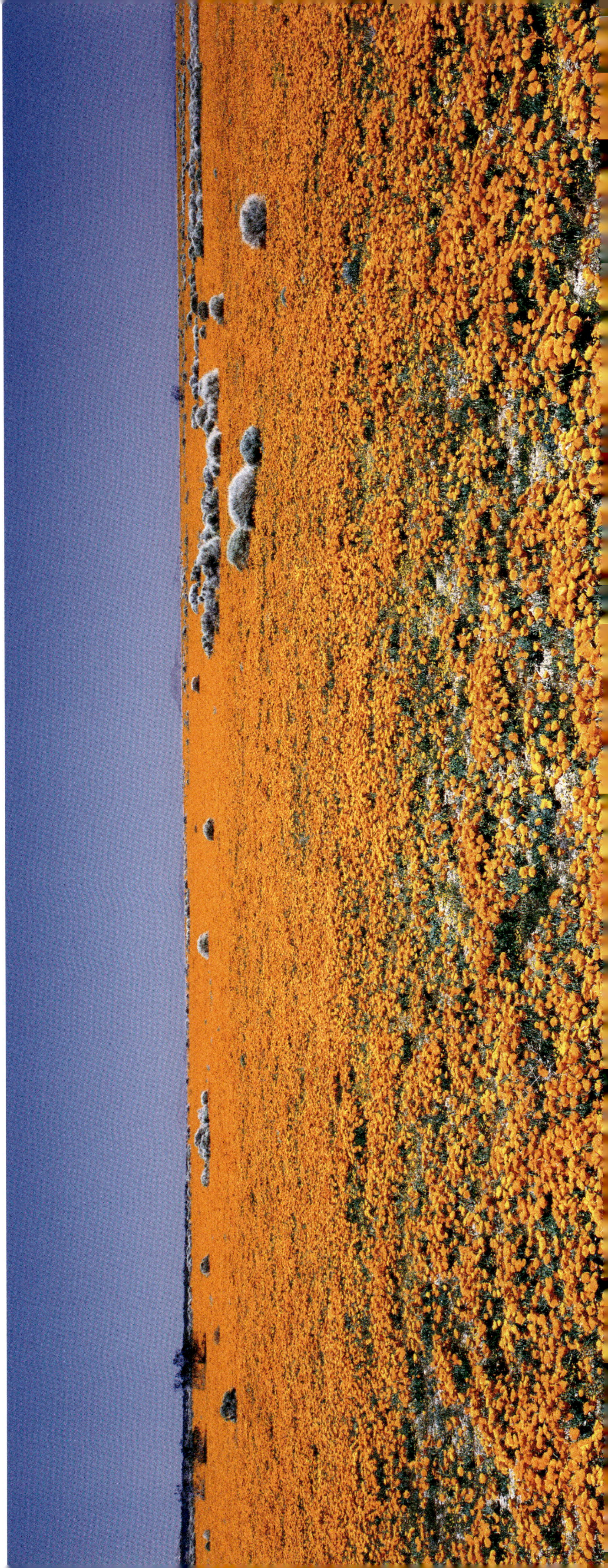

Walk of Fame, Los Angeles 49

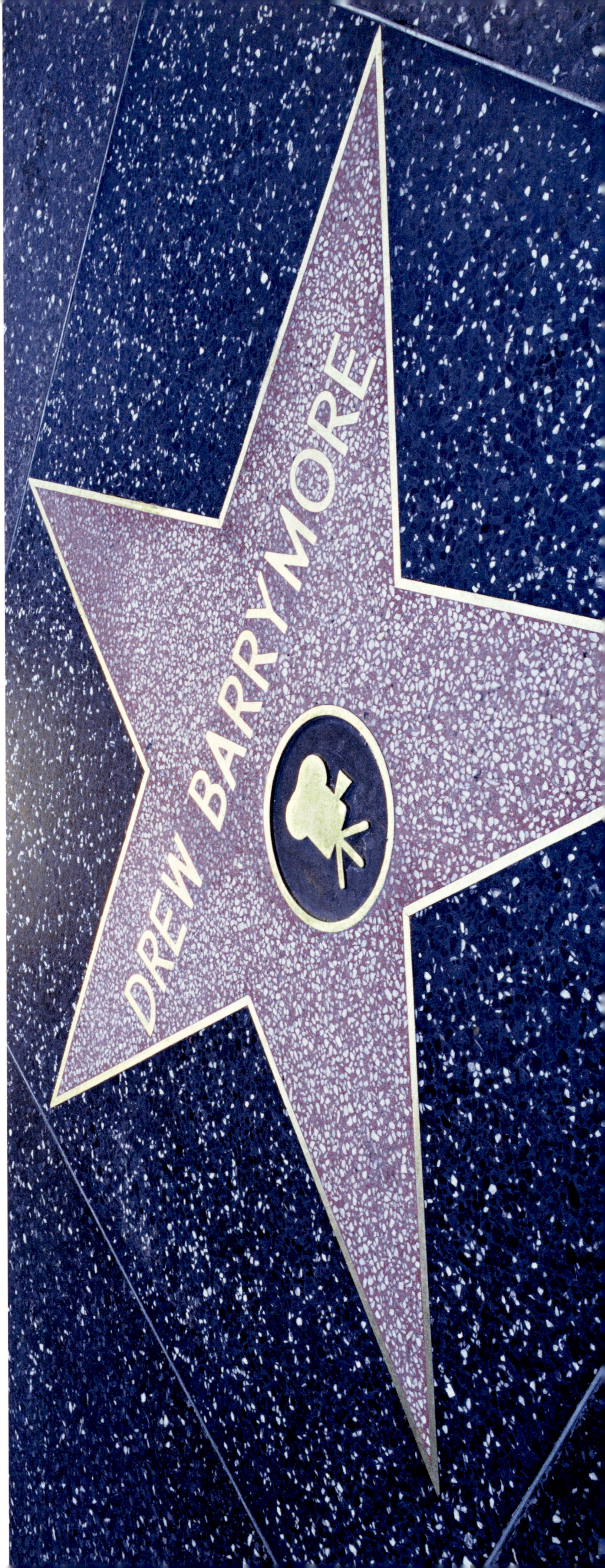
DREW BARRYMORE

J. Paul Getty Museum, Los Angeles   50

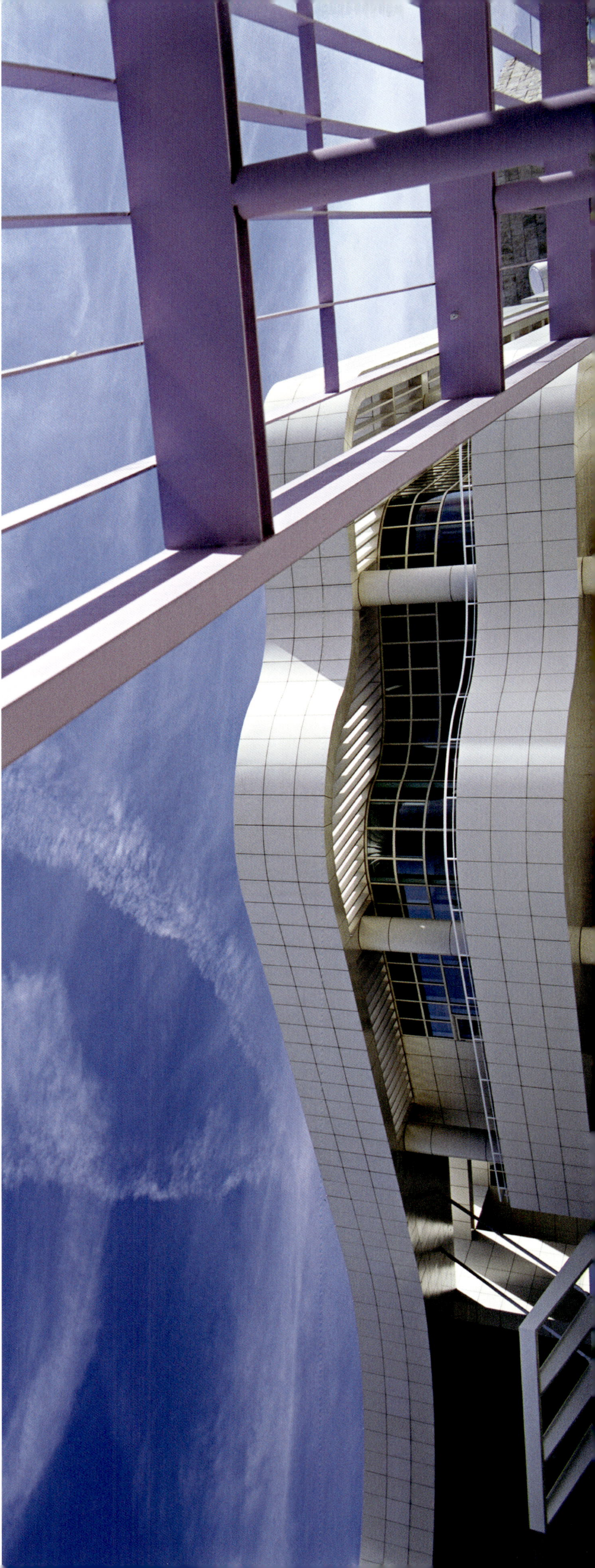

Downtown Los Angeles   51

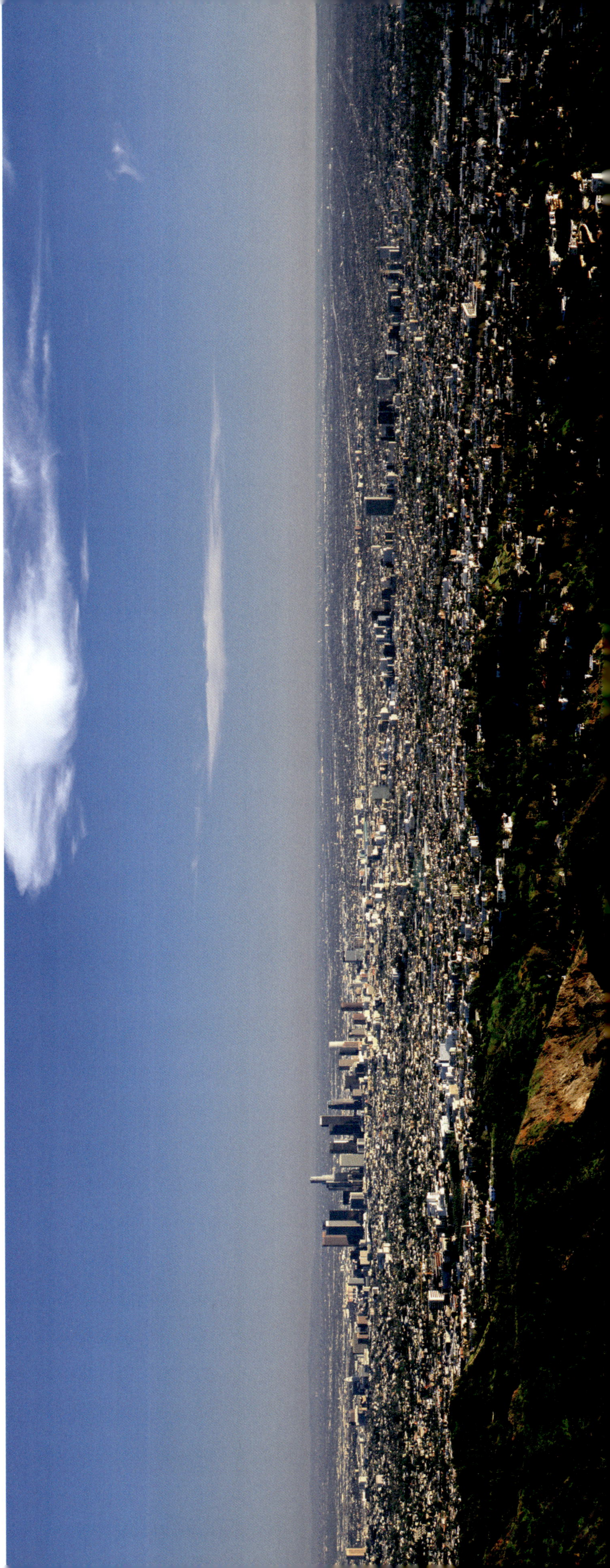

www.micha-pawlitzki.com

MICHA PAWLITZKI machte sich 1995 während seines Studiums der Betriebswirtschaft als Photograph selbständig und veröffentlichte bald erste Bildbände und Kalender. Nach Studienende, Arbeit als Dozent und Promotion in Werbepsychologie arbeitet er seit 2005 vollzeit als Photograph. Inzwischen sind über 70 Bücher und Kalender mit seinen Bildern erschienen. Micha Pawlitzki arbeitet für alle renommierten Bildagenturen und ist für seine Photoprojekte jedes Jahr vier bis fünf Monate im Ausland unterwegs. Mit seiner Frau Melanie lebt er in Augsburg.

CLAUS KLEBER gilt als einer der besten deutschen TV-Journalisten. Schon während seines Jurastudiums, das er 1986 mit einer Promotion abschloss, begann er journalistisch zu arbeiten. Ab 1992 arbeitete Kleber im ARD Studio in Washington D.C., dessen Leitung er 1997 übernahm. Im Februar 2003 wurde Claus Kleber Leiter und Moderator des „ZDF heute journal". Für seine Arbeit erhielt er mehrere deutsche Fernsehpreise. Sein Bestseller „Amerikas Kreuzzüge" wurde mit dem Internationalen Buchpreis Corine für das beste deutsche Sachbuch 2005 ausgezeichnet.

MICHA PAWLITZKI, while completing his degree in business administration, started working professionally as a photographer in 1995. Soon he published his first coffee table books and calendars. After finishing his PhD and working as assistant professor he has been working fulltime as a photographer since 2005. He has published more than 70 books and calendars. Micha Pawlitzki works for all renowned stock photo agencies and travels abroad four to five months every year working on his photographic projects. He lives in Augsburg with his wife Melanie.

CLAUS KLEBER is widely considered one of Germany's top journalists. He started his career in broadcasting while pursuing a Law degree at Tübingen University which he completed by 1986 with a Ph.D. The same year he began reporting from the USA, initially for German Public Radio (DLF). In 1992, Kleber joined the Washington bureau of ARD, the German Public Television Network, as senior correspondent. Since 2003, he has been Managing Editor and principal anchorman of „heute journal", one of Germany's leading television news programmes.

In der EDITION PANORAMA BIBLIOTHEK erhältlich | Available in the EDITION PANORAMA BIBLIOTHEK

Iceland	978-3-89823-189-5	
New York	978-3-89823-392-7	
Tibet	978-3-89823-197-8	
Cuba	978-3-89823-355-2	
La Habana, Cuba	978-3-89823-179-4	
Australia	978-3-89823-284-5	
Paris	978-3-89823-239-5	
Budapest	978-3-89823-280-7	
Jemen	978-3-89823-278-4	
Patagonia	978-3-89823-360-6	
Norway	978-3-89823-393-4	
Wien	978-3-89823-380-4	
Mallorca	978-3-89823-290-6	
Dubai	978-3-89823-279-1	
Toscana	978-3-89823-198-5	
Schwarzwald	978-3-89823-395-8	
Salzburg	978-3-89823-394-1	
Amsterdam	978-3-89823-353-8	
Berlin	978-3-89823-168-8	
Hamburg	978-3-89823-283-8	
India	978-3-89823-237-1	
New Zealand	978-3-89823-359-0	
Islas Canarias	978-3-89823-357-6	
Bruxelles	978-3-89823-354-5	
Frankfurt	978-3-89823-390-3	
Österreich	978-3-89823-381-1	
Lisboa	978-3-89823-358-3	
California	978-3-89823-389-7	
Heidelberg	978-3-89823-356-9	
Bodensee	978-3-89823-282-1	
Sylt	978-3-89823-363-7	
Venezia	978-3-89823-238-8	
Schweiz	978-3-89823-362-0	
Sahara	978-3-89823-183-1	
Roma	978-3-89823-361-3	

© 2008 EDITION PANORAMA, Germany and Micha Pawlitzki
A production by EDITION PANORAMA, Germany

All rights reserved
Printed in Germany
All photographs: © Micha Pawlitzki and EDITION PANORAMA
Text: © Claus Kleber and EDITION PANORAMA

EDITION PANORAMA GmbH
G7, 14
D-68159 Mannheim
Telefon +49 (0)621 / 32 88 69 - 0
Fax +49 (0)621 / 32 88 69 - 20
info@editionpanorama.com
www.editionpanorama.com

ISBN: 978-3-89823-389-7

Concept: Bernhard & Sebastian Wipfler
Design: EDITION PANORAMA | Diana May
Designgruppe Fanz & Neumayer | Marcus Bela Schmitt
Editorial department: Dr. Michael Barchet, Wolfgang Roth
Translations: Global-Text, Heidelberg | Mark Woolfe
Separations: EPS GmbH, Speyer
Printing: Passavia Druckservice GmbH & Co. KG, Passau
Printed on Profimatt, produced by Sappi – exclusive by Igepagroup
Bookbinding: Josef Spinner Großbuchbinderei GmbH, Ottersweier
Covermaterial: "Imperial" Book Cloth, BN International
Endpapers: "Freelife Merida Graphite" 140 g/m², Fedrigoni Group
Slipcase: Neudel Verpackungen GmbH, Neckarbischofsheim

No part of this book may be reproduced in any form or by any electronic or mechanical means without prior written permission from the publisher EDITION PANORAMA, Germany.